CONSERVATIONS
WITH
LIFE

SALLY PATCH

Conversations With Life
First published in Australia by Sally Patch 2024

A catalogue record for this
book is available from the
National Library of Australia

ISBN: 978-1-7636880-0-1 (pbk)
ISBN: 978-1-7636880-1-8 (ebk)

Typesetting and design by Publicious Book Publishing
Published in collaboration with Publicious Book Publishing
www.publicious.com.au

INTRODUCTION

You may not necessarily agree with everything that I've written in this book, that's not the point. These are my conversations and yours may well be different. No one's journey is the same or more or less important than anyone else's.

THROUGH THE WINDOW

Everybody is a window
A window on the world of life,
A different view from every one
With different hues of love and strife.

And every window has a pain
That cuts the viewer from the whole,
And every window is a hole
That has a view within its frame.

Different shapes and different sizes
Each an individual look,
And thus the tale of every one
Does make a different kind of book.

For some are blanked by heavy curtains
Some have bars and shutters too,
And some have lace or slats or drapes
Or muslin filtering the view.

But some are large and all expansive
With window seats and friendly smiles
That welcome you, that say, "How are you?"
"Stop....come here and sit awhile."

And so remember as you travel,
As your tale of life unwinds,
You can always change the view
Because the window is your mind.

Sally Patch 2001

How I came to write this book

I have lived on Beechmont for over forty years and we have had many bush fires over that time. But in September 2019 a fire many times fiercer than any previously experienced raged its way over our beautiful mountain. Many houses were burnt down. Never before had there been anything so frightening and traumatic. Some time after the fire had wreaked its havoc, I heard that a woman named Shel Sweeney was coming to hold a writing workshop in order to help people get over this shocking event.

During the workshop she asked us to imagine that we were the fire, and write something from the fire's point of view. That's when I wrote the page which I have called Bushfire. Two years later I thought, why don't I imagine myself as other entities in life and write from their points of view. That was the beginning of this book.

When I think about it though, the book really started way before that. It has been growing in my being since 1999 when I was 51..... that is the year that grief consumed me and spat me out. During the ensuing period I decided to face everything that frightens me. Consequently the view from the window of my mind changed dramatically, and is in fact still changing.

Sally Patch. 2024.

CONTENTS

1

ANXIETY

ME Hello Anxiety, you are so familiar to me. I can't remember it, but you probably first entered my life immediately after I was born, because I was rushed off to hospital without my mother to have a blood transfusion. After that, I apparently couldn't sleep and was crying constantly. For the first four years of my life I refused to eat anything solid, so Mum ended up giving me everything in a bottle. I am now wondering if all this had anything to do with you.

ANXIETY Absolutely, I relish these sort of incidences, they allow me to get a nice strong hold on my unsuspecting prey.

ME The first time that I actually remember meeting you was when I was about three or four. I was just a little girl trying to cope......

My father was a very quiet, gentle, and loving man. In the beginning I adored him. I didn't see that much of him as he was away at sea a lot, but when he came home it was like having a gentle God around the place. I think I'd put him on a bit of a pedestal, which is apparently quite a common thing for a little girl to do.

Then one day my Mum went out leaving me and my little brother in his care. My brother and I were playing a bit too enthusiastically inside our house, which was a thatched cottage the size of a pea, and he eventually got cross with us. It was the first and only time that he ever got angry with me and I was in a state of shock. I couldn't believe it, my brother was crying and my gentle God had suddenly got angry with us and was unavailable, hiding behind his newspaper as if we suddenly didn't exist. I felt abandoned, shocked, devastated, let down, and powerless. My lovely father had changed before my eyes. I lost my trust in him and so I couldn't go to him. I was too frightened, frightened of being rejected. I didn't allow myself to be close to him after that. He obviously had no idea how to cope with us or repair the relationship, and anyway by that time the wall had sprung up between us. It felt so real, it separated us, and for the next fifty-seven years I did my best to ignore him.

To make matters worse, when my Mum came home that day and found my brother crying, she went straight to him to comfort him, so the feeling of abandonment and no-one being there for me was reinforced.

The belief that I made up about my father was that I didn't need him because I couldn't trust him. The belief I made up about my mother was that I had to be a good girl so that she would love me and wouldn't ignore me ever again. Both these beliefs grew inside my mind to epic proportions, so that they controlled me. I suspect now that you were there.

I don't remember either of my parents ever telling me that they loved me. There was almost no physical affection in our family, but there was kindness, support and a great sense of loyalty.

ANXIETY I'm extremely stealthy. I often sneak into someone's life when they are a child, usually after an incident such as yours, where they end up feeling separated and alienated from their care givers. The more sensitive the child is, the easier it is for me to enter and the more traumatised they are likely to become.

ME I think that I, and probably also my brother are both quite sensitive. I would say that we are definitely not tough nuts!

The most wonderful thing about my childhood however, was my relationship with my brother. We were very close and played together constantly. He was a very daring and creative companion. We were living in the country fairly isolated from people, so we spent our days together endlessly making things out of anything that was available. My mother encouraged this with virtually no limits, and the more outrageous the ideas were the better she liked it. She maintained a very relaxed, disciplined and orderly household. This gave me a feeling of safety but I was always conscious of you; a background hum quietly vibrating, a vacuum of uncertainty, buzzing about nothing in particular but everything in general. My state of being was slightly unsure; unsure of everything. Unfortunately this was constant and so became my normal state.

Sometimes, when I was older and a challenging event occurred, like having to play the piano at school in evening prayers, or when I tried to join the choir, you'd bang your drums and sound your horns in the pit of my churning stomach. My guts would turn to liquid lead, and my hands and voice would shake uncontrollably. The rest of the time you were just there skulking shakily in the shadows.

So what are you, a lack of trust?

ANXIETY Yes indeed, I am a lack of trust in life. A timeless tuneless note that's lost its way, quavering in the darkness, searching for the light, unsure which way to go, up or down, right or left, I hover uncertainly, quavering, quivering. When the heart opens though, even for an instant, I am snuffed out like a candle in a black hole.

ME I see. I am saved by the heart, that resting place of trust. The view widens, the heart opens and you and doubt fly out the window. I am left in a paradise of knowing, where everything is crystal clear, and I am basking in a tidal wave of love.

But it never lasts, you always return.

ANXIETY I will, until I don't. Just keep watching me without any judgement, no judgement at all, and no wanting me to disappear. Be vigilant, very very vigilant, notice me when I visit you. The day will come when the tidal wave of love will come and swallow me up, never to return.

2

GRIEF

ME Hello Grief, you started it all you know, because without you in my life this series of conversations probably would never have eventuated. You have visited me four times altogether, and the third time you very nearly annihilated me.

GRIEF So let's start with the first time.

ME Actually the first time I met you I have already talked about in my conversation with Anxiety. An incident happened and I felt abandoned first by my father closely followed by my mother and my whole world fell apart. My heart was broken, I lost all trust in life and you came to visit, with Anxiety close on your heals.

GRIEF So what happened the second time?

ME That was when I was twenty two. I was in a relationship with a young man called Keith. We were at art school together. A year into our relationship he got very sick. The doctors found out that a virus had got into his heart and eaten away a valve. They eventually replaced it and three months after the operation and still in hospital, he died. I couldn't believe it at first. Every time the telephone rang I'd think it was him and then I'd remember. I'd always thought I wouldn't be able to live without him. But after he died there I was, still alive. It was somehow so mysterious, how could someone just disappear? Where was he? All these questions to which there seemed to be no answers. However, I began to suspect there was more to life than what I could actually see. Eventually, even though I missed him terribly and felt incredibly sad, I realised I had begun to feel much stronger than I ever had before, and after a year I felt able to move on.

GRIEF You see I do have my uses don't I? I made you stronger and a bit more aware. So what happened the third time you met me, the time I nearly annihilated you.

ME Well it was 1998 and I was at a New Years Eve party. I was nearly fifty and had been on my own for seventeen years. I decided this was going to be the year of romance. Straight away two men appeared and I made my choice. Here was Mr Right at last.

It was all going swimmingly for just over a year, I was in heaven. Then one day, completely out of the blue, Mr Right announced that he couldn't do it any more. He'd turned from a warm loving man into a human iceberg. He couldn't give me any reason for ending it and I was very confused and shocked. I just couldn't understand it, because it didn't make sense. The sick feeling of empty darkness, sadness, and confusion was overwhelming and incomprehensible. I couldn't get my head around what had happened. I was floundering around in a sea of misery.

What I'd thought life was about before, now seemed superfluous and meaningless. The thought of suicide flitted across my mind, but I knew I wouldn't do it, somehow I knew that wasn't the answer. There had to be a reason why this had happened.

Months passed and I kept trying to understand. One day a thought came to me, it said 'what was your part in it?' Immediately a moment of clarity hit me between the eyes and I knew that something I'd said had upset him. It was truly an epiphany. But even though some of the confusion left, my misery was as intense as ever and I still thought about him constantly. In fact, my thoughts were driving me mad.

GRIEF That's what it's like with me, when you see more of the story it's a relief isn't it? Sometimes I get so intense for you that you finally take some responsibility and that means you can see a wider picture and not just a part of it. This is so important, because in a way that's what I'm for, to whirl you off to a different view point. I'm sometimes quite a complicated phenomenon aren't I? Also, I can be really quite insistent can't I? The degree to which you feel me is related to how attached you are to the thing or person that you miss. Contrary to popular belief attachment has very little to do with love. Attachment is imprisoning whereas love is freeing.

ME Yes, your insistence is intense. Then over the next six months three quite remarkable things happened.

GRIEF Really. I'm curious. What happened?

ME   Well, the first one is really weird. It was one of those bad days when I was extra tightly wrapped in my misery. I walked out of my kitchen door wondering how to cope. I looked up at the enormous tree that stands there and I said, 'Help, I need some help.' Immediately I had this strange feeling that I was the tree. It was magical! Suddenly there was no separation, I was the tree, we were one. I turned my head slightly. I saw a bird flying across the sky, and holy dooley, I was the bird, the bird was me. This strange sense of oneness with everything was incredible. It persisted for a couple of weeks, diminishing slowly as time passed. I noticed that it was accompanied by a curious thing.

GRIEF   Which was?

ME   My mind had stopped. I'd stopped thinking about Mr Right. My mind was totally still. Empty. I was just calm and peaceful going about my business. I was happy. It was amazing. I didn't *try* not to think, I just didn't think. And for those two weeks I felt at one with things. A faint whisper wafting in the calmness seemed to be saying….***This is how it could always be.***

But no, the magic was abruptly shattered by an insistent ring. Mr Right was on the telephone. It was the only time he ever rang me after he had dumped me, and all he wanted to do was moan about his life. So I listened, and when the conversation ended I noticed, the feeling of oneness, that magical interlude, had gone. My mind had started up again and I was back in my cloak of misery.

GRIEF   I was back eh. What was the second remarkable thing that happened?

ME   Well, I was at a friend's house and I was moaning on about my confusion and misery, and my friend said to me 'Sally, I have a book here which I think you should read'. I looked up as she walked over to her enormous bookcase stretching across the whole wall. As she searched I sat there immersed in my misery. Then I looked again and saw how determined she was. I thought I suppose I should help her find it, so I said 'What's it called?', 'Sacred World' she replied, and so I got up and went over to help. Half heartedly I reached up and pulled down a book that was lying horizontally across the top of some of the others. There it was … Sacred World.

So I took it home and read it. That book opened my eyes to a whole new world, a larger spiritual world that was there all the time, but I'd never acknowledged before. Other books started flooding in from everywhere. I read incessantly. I also started walking at night. I'd walk down the road to where there were no houses or lights, lie down on the warm deserted tarmac with my dog and look up at the majesty of the night sky glittering above me. Somehow the vastness of it was very comforting. It seemed to be saying, ***it's alright, welcome to the magical mystery.***

GRIEF   So that was the second remarkable thing that happened, what was the third?

ME   Well, the thoughts of missing him still engulfed me all the time, my mind was driving me mad and I knew I needed to learn how to meditate. I tried to follow instructions in books but I knew I really needed some help. Then one day I was in a community gardening group and I was talking to a young man who was weeding the garden next to me.

He suddenly said, Sally, do you want to come to a meeting tonight? I said, What are you meeting about? He said, I'm a Steiner School teacher and I have to teach Genesis next term and I need to know a bit about it, so we are going to read the Bible. I said, Wow, that's an interesting idea, I'd love to. That meeting led to a whole year of investigating not only the Bible but a host of other reading material.

Every evening as they were getting ready to go home the young man and his friend would talk about a thing with a weird name. Eventually I asked them what it was, and they told me that it was Vipassana which is a type of meditation, and that it is taught at a retreat centre not far away. I was over joyed and two weeks later there I was. Vipassana had entered my life.

GRIEF So I took you on quite a journey there didn't I? What was the fourth time I visited you?

ME Well that was when I finally realised the truth about my relationship with my father. When I talked to Anxiety I realised that there was a wall between myself and my father.

GRIEF So what was this truth about that wall?

ME Well, I finally realised the wall that was always there between us was in fact my wall and not his. I had always thought that it was his wall.

GRIEF Ah, so you took responsibility again did you?

ME Yes, I suppose I did. The wall between us was mine and it was built out of my fear of being rejected. The relief of seeing this truth was amazing. My love for him, the love I had suppressed for all those years rose up in me like a fountain gushing everywhere. The sadness was over-whelming though. The sadness of missing him in my life for all those years was excruciating, so you were right there. I could see I had missed out on having a proper relationship with my father, because of the wall, my wall.

And there was something else as well which I have only just realised. My father lived near me for many years, and I looked after him for the last two years of his life until he finally died in my arms. During all that time I didn't realise I still had a massive fear of being rejected by him. I felt that if I allowed myself to become vulnerable enough to talk to him about our relationship he would reject me in some way. So the fear of being rejected was still controlling me. It's taken me such a long long time to realise all this. Pretty sad eh?

GRIEF Yes, that's me, sad as hell. So, you had pushed me down by making up a compelling story that wasn't really true, and you carried this story for many, many years, during which time you suffered greatly.

ME Yes, that's right I did.

GRIEF Well despite everything, I think a little thanks might be in order don't you?

ME Yes, you pushed me into a lot of realisations didn't you? It was quite a journey, very painful at times, but oh so worth it. You changed me into a completely different person. You can be a very transformative being.

GRIEF   I couldn't have done it without your co-operation you know.

ME   Well many many thanks anyway, it was a roller coaster of a ride.

3

FREEDOM

ME   Hi Freedom. It would be nice to be able to say it…..I'm Free, but somehow I know that I cannot. Not yet anyway!

FREEDOM   Why not, what's stopping you?

ME   Well, I suppose a sense of somehow being stuck in this place, this world, trapped here with all my unhelpful stories and emotions.

FREEDOM   So you feel that you are stuck in this world that you have created. It is indeed very complex, full of different organisations like governments and corporations and the like. You feel they have authority over you, and when you feel that something has authority over you I am banished from your consciousness and replaced by fear or anxiety, which also seem to have authority over you.

Also there is still a lot of violence in your world which generates fear. To find me, work towards saying no to all authority, and instead apply all your efforts to realising exactly who you are. Find out all about yourself. Take responsibility for all that you have created in your life. Go within and enquire and keep enquiring until a completeness is obtained. You will know because you will find me, you will feel that nothing is holding you in check, no fear, need, anger or any other negative emotion is binding you.

Acceptance is my friend, *you cannot change anyone else, only yourself.*

ME   I see, and wow, you said I created it, this world of conflict. And now I feel as though I'm here to learn lessons by looking within and finding what is really true, but the lessons seem to be going on and on and on. I sometimes feel as though it's all getting me nowhere. And yet, at other times, I feel as though I'm on top of the world, it's weird. Some of the lessons seem to be about my beliefs and whether they are true or false. When I realise they are false and that they are imprisoning me, that very awareness is what frees me from them. That's when I feel on top of the world. There also seems to be things that are buried deeper within. It just feels like it's never-ending.

FREEDOM   So there's another belief, eh, it's never-ending. Is it really, and does it matter anyway? *In fact I am always in the present moment.* Whenever you allow your mind to go out of the present moment into either the past or the future, that's when you are truly trapped, and you've lost me. Say goodbye to that fictitious flighty friend of yours called Time, and come back my friend, to me. Ask yourself what is it that takes you out of the present moment, what takes you away from me? You said it already….. those beliefs; all that conditioning cluttering up your mind. Some from eons gone by, are fears, held within your body as sensations. If you project them into the future, and they stop you from doing things, they have you in their grasp, and you lose me. Other thoughts are dreams, desires of future things, held too tightly, with too much wanting. I like a bit of flow, so **no attachment to outcome is very important.**

Taking action on something you have fear of doing is powerful, and often you will find that it's not as scary as you thought it would be, and more of me is suddenly available. Live life as an adventure, but don't forget to observe yourself while acting on something. Always be self aware. Sensations in the body are the key, observe them closely, **without any outcome for them in mind**, just pure observing.

ME Yes some of them are so powerful, so strong, they seem to have such a hold on me. The habit of dropping into them is very compulsive, they have such a grip on me. I notice that I often wake up with fear in my body..... it's strange. I have no idea what it's about, it's just there, sensations in my stomach, or in my gut. I asked my Meditation teacher what to do about it and she said, observe objectively. So I do.

FREEDOM Good. Keep observing. Sometimes the only action needed, is to just .... observe, to be aware. **Silent, intense observation has great power.** You underestimate it massively, probably because it has no drama.

Many times there are no words or story behind the sensations. Like your fear in the morning when you wake up, they are just sensations held within the body. All your past traumas are held within your body as sensations. Observe the sensations silently without any wanting, without any aversion, without any motive. Silent passive observation, that's all. ***The more you know yourself the more I will be with you.*** So just observe. Everything changes, so the sensations will pass .... and come again .... and pass .... and come again .... and pass .... and come again .... until they don't. The more you know yourself the more I will be present.

4

ANGER

ME   You're a full on character aren't you?

ANGER   Well actually in my pure form I'm just energy, powerful undefiled energy. A good thing when utilised correctly, because I can generate action. Unfortunately, some of you are quite often using that energy in a very negative way, either against someone else or against yourself, and that's when that energy is me. I can then create much chaos and heartbreak. When a lot of you get together and use me, I can unfortunately help you to create so much conflict it can sometimes escalate into a war. It's not my fault really though, I'm just an energy.

ME   Yes I can see that? Tell me more.

ANGER   Well, think about it for a minute. Something happens that you don't like, you react negatively and then I rise up from where I've been lurking in your body, and sometimes I spew out all over the place. If you're alert and aware enough you can feel me, because I produce all sorts of different sensations in your body, sensations like, heat, agitation, shaking, tension and also, blindness to the misery within yourself. When you're reacting blindly you start flinging me around like a hand grenade, so that I affect everybody around you in some way.

I always start in the mind, with a reactive thought. I recommend you observe that crazy mind of yours more closely, and see how those unruly thoughts affect your body. They wake me up big-time.

Next time something happens that you don't like, try observing what is going on in your mind and body. I'm easy to spot, I don't hide myself very well, I am a very powerful energy. The sensations that I create in your body are really quite obvious, the challenge is to notice me *without reacting*, to feel me, to observe me objectively, and to keep feeling me until I'm gone. I have to confess, making you react is quite fun really. I can make you think, say and do all sorts of unhelpful things when you're reacting blindly and not being aware! I sometimes can't believe I get away with it so easily, I'm such a blatant little devil.

Awareness is the key to recognising me before I get out of hand. It needs to be just awareness though, *with absolutely no wanting to change anything*. Remember, if you observe me intensely enough, with no need to alter me, I can change in an instant and become pure flowing energy, ready for you to use in a more helpful, creative and inspiring way. So...next time you feel me arrive, instead of reacting blindly, see if you can just observe those sensations in your body objectively, with no judgement and no wanting them to change.

For children it's a bit different as they may not have learnt how to be aware enough yet. There are several ways that adults can help them to be more at home with me. Firstly never stop them from having me, instead help them to accept me, allow them to have their out bursts, remember I am just energy, and can be extremely useful if handled correctly. So allow them to feel me, to experience me without making them wrong. Encourage them to punch pillows, stamp their feet, run round the house or garden, scream into a pillow, anything to use me up without destruction being involved.

ME I know from my own experience that it is very important for a child to be able to fully express their emotions without being squashed, even if they are very negative and disruptive. My son and daughter-in-law live with me, and their second child, a daughter named Layla, is a very strong willed child. She was subject to many screaming sessions every day, which often lasted for hours. They never reprimanded her when she was having a tantrum, but did their best to tolerate her out bursts and be present with her while waiting for them to finish. She is now five and although she is still quite challenging, she is turning into a very interesting, happy, funny and likeable human being. There seem to be many more extreme cases of this sort of behaviour now days, calling for extreme tolerance and love. It must be very difficult for these parents. Somewhere along the line we seem to have lost the art of tolerance, and replaced it with the need for people to conform, not disturb others and have good manners.

ANGER I do present quite a challenge you know, because I am extremely powerful and potent. However the rewards for your perseverance in this are enormous. My energy is vast and can be so beneficial when handled correctly. So when I next rise up in you, remember to shine your lights on me, your lights of awareness and equanimity. Get to know me more intimately, I promise you won't regret it.

5

ALCHEMY

ME   I am curious, because I feel like I already know you…..

ALCHEMY   You do, because I am the ultimate magic trick, and without me you wouldn't be here. My tools are awareness, concentration and focus. Pure unadulterated awareness, concentration and laser-like focus, with not even a smidgen of any wants or needs, but with a mind open to all and anything.

ME   You must be very powerful?

ALCHEMY   You are too, you've just forgotten.

ME   So what do I focus on?

ALCHEMY   Whatever is going on within your body; thoughts, sensations, feelings, allow your awareness to sear into them, just notice them and let them be.

ME   Wow, that reminds me of an incident that happened to me. I wonder if I can tell you about it, so that you can tell me if it had anything to do with you?

ALCHEMY   Certainly, fire away then.

ME   I was with a boy of about nine named Charlie, I suggested we play a card game called Uno. We started playing and he kept changing the rules to suit himself. I found this really frustrating. I started challenging him by telling him to stop. He didn't like this. Eventually he said in a very firm, low, menacing voice, 'You're making me very angry'. By this time I could feel my own anger rising up. It was so powerful that I was actually shaking with it. So I started observing it as it pulsated in my body, because I remembered that's what I'd been told to do at the meditation retreat, observe it objectively with no judgement of myself for having it, and no wanting to get rid of it, just pure observation.

Charlie looked as though he was going to explode at any minute. Our anger was so powerful. It seemed to hang there, oscillating between us. I remember thinking it's all right Sally, just concentrate on the sensations. I'm not sure exactly how it happened, but I know we were looking at each other intensely and then one, or perhaps both of us, smiled and in that moment the energy changed! Suddenly, we were laughing and chasing each other around the house. It was so funny how the anger dissolved and turned into that crazy hilarious energy. We were both bursting with it, and it felt wonderful. A huge amount of love for him rose up in me, and I think that it affected him in the same way. He was shining with it. I could feel tremendous love flowing between us. It was quite magical and very joyful. Anger dissolved into joy. I am so grateful to him, because it was so powerful.

Do you think you were involved in that?

ALCHEMY   Absolutely, that is how it works. One thing changes into another, and you're right, like I said, *I am magical, life is magical*. Most people have just forgotten. Remember though, do not crave me, do not *try* to have me, or you'll never even catch a glimpse of me.

6

RESPONSIBILITY, FORGIVENESS and COMPASSION

RESPONSIBILITY The question is, are you taking me seriously….. are you taking responsibility?

ME For what exactly?

RESPONSIBILITY For the things that happen in your life.

ME Do you mean I am responsible for everything that happens in my life?

RESPONSIBILITY Let's look at it a little more closely and see.

ME So like, what if someone runs into me in my car, am I responsible?

RESPONSIBILITY Whose choices led you to be there at that particular time?

ME Mine I suppose.

RESPONSIBILITY So does that make you responsible?

ME I used to think this was so, but I have come to realise it involves two of us so we both may have parts in it. It's really up to both of us to become aware of our share of you.

RESPONSIBILITY That's right. If you had been more aware at the time, in other words if you had been totally present, aware of everything going on around you, would you have got out of the way?

ME Of course I would, if it was possible, but sometimes it just isn't possible.

RESPONSIBILITY In that case, it would be his fault. For you though, in any situation there is always an opportunity for some new awareness, it doesn't matter how much pain there is, or how little you are to blame. You miss out if you are not aware. Usually the solution to the situation will have something to do with forgiveness either of yourself or the other.

ME Really, but what if I was raped, or molested as a very young child?

RESPONSIBILITY If someone does something to another person without their permission, that is an act of violence. They are a perpetrator. Rape is a particularly violent act, and so that person must be carrying an awful lot of violence within themselves to be able to do that. Children are very vulnerable as they may not have had the chance to become self aware. Forgiveness is still the road to freedom though, and though an enormous challenge, it is certainly not impossible.

ME   I have found that when 'bad' things have happened in my life the question has always arisen, 'Does life happen *to* me, or does life happen *for* me? If my answer is, life happens *to* me, it can easily make me feel like a victim. If my answer is, life happens *for* me, then it feels as though life is a gift which opens up a whole host of other questions. Questions like, why could that experience possibly be for my benefit? How can I possibly find some forgiveness? Did I unwittingly invite it into my life in any way?

Did I choose my life, or is my life just some random thing that happens without any reason or plan, the luck of the draw as it were? Is my life chosen for me? Do we come here to learn lessons? If so, do we choose what we need to learn? What was my part in it? It requires a great deal of self reflection to be able to see any answers. But if life happens for us it stands to reason that there must be some lessons and some answers.

RESPONSIBILITY   Remember, when you look deeply into the incident and find you are to blame, either fully or in part, you then have an opportunity to make amends as best you can and to find forgiveness for yourself. This may involve some very intense self reflection and you may need help with this. When you succeed in your search for forgiveness, your power will come rushing back instantly, and you are no longer at the mercy of your life. Instead you become the driver of your life. Your sense of freedom increases dramatically.

What do you think Forgiveness?

FORGIVENESS   I am always available, you just have to find me, and like you say, self reflection is the way.

ME   So what if I look and realise I had no opportunity for escaping the situation, and I am an innocent victim, is this when I need to forgive the person who has hurt me, because if I don't forgive them then I am not free?

FORGIVENESS   That's right, I am the bringer of freedom, and I'll be right there if you look. How is it possible to find both me and compassion for someone who mistreats you, someone who hurts you really really badly?

ME   I have found that every trauma that has ever happened to me is held within my body as sensations. Therefore, I would say becoming aware of and observing all the sensations and feelings that come up for us within our bodies and learning to be equanimous with them is very important. There will be many feelings and sensations following any traumatic incident. I've found that observing them objectively and intensely is when the alchemy happens. That's when things can be transformed. That's when the compassion arises.

Do not forget though that observing intensely has to be done without any wanting of a particular result, or actually any result whatsoever. It has to be just observation. Pure observation. Objective observation. It's the ability for intense observation that is important. The mind coming in and putting demands on the situation will negate your efforts.

Some people may think the perpetrator gets off scot free though. Responsibility what do you think?

RESPONSIBILITY Is that really true? He/she still has to live with themselves knowing what they've done, and that would be no easy task at all. Remember though, they too always have the opportunity of going within to find forgiveness for themselves.

FORGIVENESS That's right, I am available to all, no one is exempt. Some people have this big belief in punishing people, as if it's going to make everything all right. Really the only thing that makes anything right is me. Ponder all this and we all wish you much focus, deep delving and hopefully some breath taking moments of clarity.

Compassion you are very quiet, perhaps you would like to say something.

COMPASSION I am the ability to feel what it's like to be someone else, to walk in their shoes, and to know how human it is. I arise through my friend Forgiveness. I am felt in your heart.

7

AWARENESS versus SELF-IMPROVEMENT

ME Hi Awareness, what's going on, is there a problem?

AWARENESS Well sort of. Self-Improvement says I make it all sound too easy. My main thing is that I just am, that is it. I have no sense of becoming, no sense of getting rid of something, no sense of condemnation, I am the silent mind, the silent witness, just observing what is. So in order to have more of me in your life, just notice how you're feeling in any situation without any judgement at all, without it needing to be different from how it is.

Notice how your body feels, notice all its sensations with no judgement. Notice whether your mind is being very balanced and equanimous with everything that is going on. Notice if it wants something to be different, and bring it back to the present. Be very passive, even while you're doing, with no wants and no desire for anything to be different, with no aversion and no judgement. I am so simple and uncomplicated, just content to watch and see what happens without a specific end in mind.

SELF-IMPROVEMENT Really? That sounds just too easy and rather boring, you're not busy enough, you'll get nowhere.

AWARENESS   Is there anywhere to get to?

SELF-IMPROVEMENT   Well of course there is! I'm angry and I don't like it, I want to be peaceful and I want to be successful.

AWARENESS   Well just try this, observe your anger and your desire to be sucsessful and at peace. When they come, silently observe them objectively, with no motive to make them different, no judgement to squash them and no wishing to make them disappear. Welcome them and just observe intensely, give them a wink and a nod. They're just energy kicking their heals up. Allow them to run their course. When you want them to be different you just create more friction, more angst for yourself.

SELF-IMPROVEMENT   Huh, if it's that easy why aren't we all doing it? What about all those other people out there? It doesn't look very like they are doing it and a lot of them are violent. I'll be in danger.

AWARENESS   OK Self-Improvement, don't get your knickers in a knot, calm down, relax, everything is OK, quite OK the way it is, that's their business not yours. So you think you will be in danger, but will you? Sometime in the future, maybe and maybe not, but certainly not right now, not right in this moment.

I suggest you bring your mind back into the present. Don't worry about others, they're just doing their thing. Concentrate on yourself, I never said it was easy, but it's a good challenge.

SELF-IMPROVEMENT   But if we all just sit around being aware, nothing will get done.

AWARENESS   I didn't say, just sit around, I said observe yourself. Observe your body and your mind. Observe yourself while you're doing, working, making decisions, talking, playing and just sitting around. But most of all observe yourself when you are reacting, when you are in conflict with others. Observe yourself without seeking any result, with no judgement of being good or bad, be kind to yourself. Observe your body, observe your mind. And when your mind goes spinning off, into all its merry likes and dislikes, its fears, wants and desires, just notice what it's doing, and calmly, with a smile, bring it back into the present, and, remember, be kind to yourself.

SELF-IMPROVEMENT   Yes right, well I'm not entirely sure, but I'll have a go.

AWARENESS   Just remember that when you're using me you are actually meditating. Just keep focussing on the sensations in the body. The sensations are how and where our reactions are stored in our bodies. If you want to find out more about meditation, go and ask him, I'm sure he'd be delighted to help you.

8

AGRICULTURE

ME I was watching a programme on the television the other day called War on Waste. Farmers were saying that they have to plough a lot of their vegetables back into the soil or else feed it to their cows because they are the wrong size or shape; they are not perfect enough for the supermarkets to accept them! What kind of madness is that?

AGRICULTURE It does seem as though you have descended into some sort of system of madness doesn't it? Before I came along a very simple way of life existed throughout the world, where the people lived in tribes, close to nature, in tune with all around. It was obviously a very wise way to live as it lasted at least sixty thousand years. They lived in all areas of the land, some of which were quite dry, and they were healthy and strong, which is testified by photographs taken by the early invaders.

ME So it was you wasn't it, that started this craziness?

AGRICULTURE Was it? Who dreamed me up then?

ME Ah yes that was us. We had this bright idea that instead of hunting and gathering we could grow everything just the way we wanted it.

AGRICULTURE Was a little control involved there I wonder, instead of the trust, thanks and reverence that had always existed before? Actually I had always existed in a limited way in conjunction with a Hunter Gathering life-style.

ME Ahhhhhhhh maybe.

AGRICULTURE So what followed on from there?

ME In one particular corner of the world, which was known as the Fertile Crescent the people ceased to Hunt and Gather. They decided that they were going to grow all their own food, so of course more and more land was needed, and not just any old land, fertile land. A few squabbles arose over who could use the land and all of a sudden *Ownership* was dreamed up. Then, because we had to be in the same place to work the land, notice that word crept in there.....*Work*, we dreamed up the idea of houses. *Comfort* was born and building was suddenly required, so more *Work*. People started getting defensive about their land and the word *My* was born. This is *My* land. Because we were able to store the food in buildings, we decided that it would be a good idea to lock it up so no one else would get it, and then we would be able to exchange it for other things and so *Trade* was born. Finally *Money* was dreamed up. That created a lot of *Competition* within the communities, along with more, yes you've guessed it..... *Work*. At some point they also decided that it would be a good idea to grow what is now known as *Mono* crops. So they covered vast areas of land with a single crop, something that had never been done before. Mono crops is actually anti nature, because nature works on biodiversity, each species having their place. So now that they had large areas covered with the same crop, they needed **Fertilisers** to restore the land and **Poisons** to kill all the unhelpful insects who had suddenly found themselves cast out of the natural food chain. Anyway, now they could grow masses of food and have large stocks of it all stored away. This made rich people feel very **Powerful**, and the rest feel a bit like they're caught in a trap, though they eventually got used to it until it felt normal. The trap got bigger and more complicated so the powerful ones needed more and more ways to control everything and keep people in order, like governments, laws, corporations, banking, prisons and so on.

AGRICULTURE   So the system was in place and you were stuck in it. I also inadvertently produced an over whelming growth in population, didn't I? Remember that the hunter gatherers were living in tune with the land, and so they knew how many mouths the surrounding countryside could feed and adapted accordingly. Whereas when I came along you could just work hard and grow more food and then you could have more children. Interesting isn't it? Apparently that's how it works, more food, more children. So I (or rather you) did start a rather crazy descent into madness.

ME   The madness of Ownership, Competition, Money, Work, Possessions, Power, Division into rich and poor, Population Explosion and finally of course, **War**.

AGRICULTURE   Yes, so what's next?

ME   One day, quite a long time ago, I was working alongside my brother. Out of the blue he suddenly said to me, 'Sally, you know what? I think the world could be just one great big thought'.

The world stopped for an instant as that idea crashed into me, and I said, 'Yes I think you could be right'.

AGRICULTURE Well I was started with a thought wasn't I, an idea? And I seem to have brought out a lot of feelings and reactions in you all, like acquisition, control, fear, ambition, possessions, work, comfort and security or the lack of it. Maybe the invitation is to look at some of those things in yourselves, question yourselves. Then you might find that you have some hope of turning the descent into madness into a cycle of awareness, a cycle of realisation. After all life is very circular isn't it? Look at nature, everything is born, the seed is sown, then it grows into whatever it's going to be. Stems, leaves, buds, flowers and seeds are formed, then the plant grows old and withers. The leaves, stalks and flowers with all their seeds fall back into the earth where the leaves, stalks and flowers turn into new soil and the seeds sprout forth again. It's like this with everything. Remember though, each of you can do the work of looking and questioning for yourselves. You can only change yourselves, you can't change anyone else. Change yourselves and the world around you will change.

Talking about change. Maybe you just need a new idea, a new inspirational vision for how to live in the world. Tribal ways obviously worked brilliantly, so is there a way where you can live more tribally in the present environment by organising things slightly differently? Perhaps you won't need to throw me out completely, rather utilise me differently along more tribal lines. Human beings fare much better living in communities, as long as they find out how to live together without conflict. It seems that therein lies some of your troubles. Ethnic tribal people had many wise ways of how to live without conflict. Maybe it would be wise to find out more about how they did it.

ME It's funny you should say that about life being circular, and it all arises with a thought. I wonder if that is what the first people called 'The dreaming'?

AGRICULTURE They did know a thing or two I think. It's a shame you didn't take more notice. It's never too late to look inside yourselves though, the circle of life is large and inclusive.

9

BUSHFIRE

ME   Hey fire, how are you now, how do you feel?

FIRE   I'm all burnt out. It was huge and I couldn't stop it once I'd started. I got fanned by the wind and all dried up by the temperature, and it made me feel wild, like an untamed animal. Anger was there for sure, anger because no-one had looked after anything, the trees, the debris, the undergrowth were easy pickings. And so, I raged on through, without a care, without thinking, enjoying the exhilaration and the trail of black soot and scorched flesh that I left behind. Now I feel totally spent, empty like a vacant room, silent and unrepentant, because it was time.

In fact it was way way past time, because I can be utilised if managed with love and understanding, to cleanse the land, to fertilise it with my wonderful charcoal, and to initiate the opening of some seeds. All this, simply generated by a nice cool burn. Think about it everybody and learn from the ones who know.

10

CLEVERNESS and WISDOM

ME   You are both actually quite different aren't you?

CLEVERNESS and WISDOM   Yes we are.

CLEVERNESS   I am born through thinking and looking outside.

WISDOM   And I am born through silence and looking inside, though sometimes we do work together.

ME   So Wisdom, you are born when thought stops. And Cleverness, you are born when thought is focussed on an idea.

WISDOM   That's right, and we both have our place, though if you use Cleverness without me, you can get yourselves into all sorts of pickles, as you are now experiencing I believe.

CLEVERNESS   Yes I need you Wisdom, to keep me on the straight and narrow, otherwise I may get carried away with myself and chaos can take over, which is not a good thing as chaos is a very unruly being.

WISDOM I think I was more obvious in Hunter Gatherer times when life was simpler and Cleverness hadn't blown himself up to such monumental dimensions.

CLEVERNESS I didn't mean to, honestly, I didn't.

WISDOM I know, but never-the-less, things were kept in good order on the earth when the Hunter Gatherers were in charge. That's why their way of life lasted for such a long long time; sixty thousand years or more. Hunter Gathers were content. They lived by a set of lores that they took very seriously. Do no harm, Leave the earth the same, or better than you found it. Treat everybody and everything with respect.

They looked upon the earth as their Mother and knew they had to work with her, look after her and celebrate her and all she contained. They, especially the men, had many rites of passage through which they had to pass, these ceremonies were a very important part of life and could go on for many days. The men had to go through great pain with circumcision and ritual cutting. They also had to step out of their comfort zone by going on journeys to unknown places. These two things often inspired them to receive me as I often appear after periods of great pain and uncertainty

Power was not looked up to. If anyone tried to put themselves above anyone else in any way they were laughed at by the others. Competition was not a part of their life. They knew they had to get on together to survive. Co-operation was paramount. When there was conflict and differences of opinion, they had many ways of diffusing the situations without resorting to violence.

Children were brought up differently too. They knew that children were often very strong willed and needed to vent their feelings. Consequently, if a child was having a tantrum it was tolerated and sometimes even cheered on causing great mirth amongst the adults present. This allowed the children to express their feelings safely without feeling they were wrong. They were accepted for who they were, fiery or not.

ME   I have a friend in England called Mark Edwards who is a photographer. He took pictures all over the world for his environmental 'Hard Rain Project' in the 1970's. During that time he lived with many different Hunter Gatherer tribes. I asked him once what was the most striking thing that he noticed about the way they lived. He told me it was the fact that ***they had the happiest children he'd ever seen anywhere.***

I wonder if the contentment and happiness of children in a society is a measure of you, Wisdom, in their particular society? If so, Western cultures are lacking you terribly, as the rates of childhood mental illness are the highest they have ever been.

WISDOM   That is true and awfully sad as I will be right there in a flash if you start looking within more often. Cleverness has his place, but as I said before if you neglect me and just focus on him, you'll get yourselves into all sorts of pickles, childhood mental problems being just one of them. I could make a list, but I think that it's much more powerful if you realise everything for yourselves.

11

HEMP

ME Well hemp, how do you feel in this day and age?

HEMP Here I am, ignored, unused, unappreciated, maligned and judged as a criminal. Think of all the many positive properties that I engender....Lets face it, I can be used to make so many things, here's a list:

- Really well insulated house bricks.
- Strong rope, string, sacks, clothes and tents.
- In the 1930's Henry ford made what he called and Organic Car out of me, which could also be fuelled by me. This car was very difficult to break even with a sledge hammer. If you can make a car out of me it means that I would also be good for making a lot of other things that are currently made out of metal, like fridges and washing machines.
- Medicine.
- Food, I contain all the essential amino and fatty acids and am the most complete protein to be found in the vegetable kingdom, therefore I amvery nutritious for humans. I am also extremely yummy.
- Deliciously soft textiles for clothing, bed linen and the like.

And you'll be delighted to know that I am extremely easy to grow. I require minimal fertiliser and water, unlike my greedy cousin cotton, who needs masses of both, and I can also grow two crops a year which is a big bonus for you. I am really puzzled as to why you are not growing me everywhere.

And OK, it is true there is one variety of me that is hallucinatory, but whose choice is it to imbibe me? Whose responsibility is that? Surely not mine, after all, I'm just here doing my thing.

So here I am tossed aside like a lonely sock, and replaced by the razzle dazzle and shine of artificial material, and the expense and land degradation of steel, and some really toxic medicine.

And remember, when I'm finished growing what do I do? I lay down and quietly disintegrate, folding my goodness back into the earth, surrendering to the worms, insects and microbes, becoming one again with nature, unlike my gaudy plastic replacements who hang around like a bad smell, poisoning the environment.

All I need is for man to give me more of a chance to show my true colours, and prove to you all what a truly amazing asset I could be to the future of the world.

12

PLASTIC

ME   So plastic, what have you got to say for yourself in your defence?

PLASTIC   Well your honour, not much really, but is it actually my fault?

Who fell in love with me in the first place? Surely it was you humans with your love of ease and convenience.

I didn't ask to be sucked out of the ground, heated, boiled and mucked around with. I was quite happy where I was, quietly relaxing in the bowels of the earth in my natural state, which of course was oil.

Sure I may be very useful for some things and seemingly irreplaceable, but at what cost? I say seemingly because nothing is irreplaceable is it? What is the cost of ignorance? What is the cost of ignoring the consequences, of tampering with a harmless substance and then putting him on a pedestal and raising him to a Godly status?

Just look at the amount of stuff you've made, and most of it gets thrown away and creates mountains of poisonous rubbish either buried out of sight on the land, clogging up the rivers or swirling around in the sea. What are the governments doing? Are they asleep at the wheel or something? Even most of your clothes are made of me, it's ridiculous, after all, there are a lot of natural materials that you could be using. Plus you don't seem to even know how to recycle me or safely dispose of me. At least put a tax on me and make me expensive, then maybe some of you would sit up and start being sensible. Perhaps the government should think about actually banning me so I can stop being so destructive, that would be a relief.

I think you can now see what you've inadvertently let me do to the the planet since you dug me out of my comfort zone and sent me out on the loose.

ME Yes I can absolutely see that, and I can also see we need to reduce or preferably eliminate you completely, but are we willing to make the sacrifices needed?

PLASTIC Am I also a lesson in giving great thought to the consequences of all your cleverness?! Just because you can doesn't mean you should.

13

BOUNDARIES

ME   What exactly are you for?

BOUNDARIES   Basically I make people feel safe. I am especially important for young children.

ME   Why is that?

BOUNDARIES   Because being in the world is quite an intense experience, especially at first. While children are learning how to negotiate their way around the place I can be very helpful, ideally with Wisdom and Love in attendance. If children do not know me the world can be a very scary place for them. However, please make sure that they are healthy versions of me. There's a big difference between keeping a child feeling safe and putting him in a prison, even if that prison is your home.

Ultimately I allow a child to step out into the world with confidence, because when a child feels safe, he is able to venture out without feeling afraid.

ME   So what is the best way to know what our boundaries are and how to implement them with love and firmness?

BOUNDARIES   Ask yourself a lot of questions.

Sample questions are:

Who is in charge? Is it you or are you going to allow the child to think he is? If you choose the second option, please know that it can lead to a lot of insecurity for him/her, which straight away can breed irrational fears. Children who think that they are the boss are operating under a lot of very unnecessary stress.

What behaviour am I comfortable with? In other words what am I willing to let my child do and what am I unwilling for him/her to do, and am I clear about this?

Am I consistent? Or am I apt to give in, to allow something one time and not another. This is very confusing for the child and breeds distrust, which is very sad. Whereas consistency leads to stability and confidence.

Am I strong in my directions, but at the same time loving? In other words can I say no with authority, or do I have reservations. Am I having feelings of fear or unhelpful stories about staying no?

Does my child listen and hear me? Is he/she looking at you when you are speaking? Is he/she giving you his/her attention or is he/she ignoring you?

Do I feel a bit wobbly or get angry when I am asking something of him/her? Is fear controlling you? If so what are you frightened of?

Does my child appear to manipulate the situation? His need to manipulate or control springs out of anxiety. Why is he anxious, does he think that he is in charge? Wow, that's a lot of responsibility for his little shoulders.

ME I think I was very lucky with my Mum. She was a great believer in you, and we knew what was acceptable and what wasn't according to her. At the same time she encouraged us to do whatever we wanted within reason. I have to say though that my brother and I were both quite co-operative children, so she wasn't challenged much until her grand children came along.

BOUNDARIES Yes some children need much more of me than others. This means that there are extra challenges for the parents. Remember that all will be solved with consistency of me together with acceptance of the child exactly as he/she is. This of course requires angelic qualities in the parent, but you wouldn't have been given this particular child unless you were capable. We all get the challenges we need. If, as a parent you are struggling with me, find out why. Your child is giving you an opportunity, challenging but ultimately potentially amazing. You will be so glad that you took up the challenge. By the way, being loving doesn't mean you always have to be nice to your child when you don't mean it. Authenticity is the key. Beware of any tendency to pretend. The child will sense it, which will undermine the trust he has in you. So if you feel like screaming now and again, do it. While you are doing it, it is very important to stay in your own space. Do not direct it at the child. You are just showing him/her that you have big feelings as well and can become emotionally dysfunctional too.

ME   You are important for us all throughout our lives aren't you, not just when we are children?

BOUNDARIES   Absolutely. In a way though I am made to be broken. Eventually a child will grow and burst through me. He will spread his/her wings and fly out into the world, stretching himself into places he'd never thought he would go. He will do this with confidence if he has grown up with me firmly in place, together with large helpings of love. I am essential however in any relationship. You'll know that I'm probably needed when you feel uncomfortable about something that is happening between you and another.

You may think that I am very separating but actually the opposite is the case. When you are comfortable with me, it is possible for you to relate better to anyone you meet. This is because you are more likely to know how you feel, and how you want the relationship to progress. You may get into situations where you need to protect yourself in some way, to withdraw a little, or even separate yourself completely for some reason. Learn to use me wisely, but also be willing to let go of me in order to be vulnerable when appropriate. Learn to be discerning about life and especially people. Remember to question everything especially your beliefs, for beliefs can lead you down many a tricky rabbit hole.

14

EDUCATION and CONDITIONING

ME   Right you two, I would like to know more about you both please.

EDUCATION   Well at present in most schools I sometimes lead to confusion and war, because my focus is often on ambition, 'to get ahead', to compete, to be the best, to come out on top. This makes some of you feel very insecure, because any sort of competition can breed fear. So underneath your life there might run an undercurrent of fear. Fear of losing something. Fear of not being good enough. Fear of failure etcetera. Those of you who are successful generally own/win more, and so then their fear is exacerbated by the fear of losing what they have. There is nothing wrong with coming top as long as there's no attachment to it. Unfortunately, you idolise competition, mainly because it breeds excitement and is actually quite addictive. All this means that the qualities of co-operation, looking after each other and love are often rather swept under the carpet. The balance is lost.

I desperately need to change my focus because love arises through complete acceptance of yourselves, warts and all. This complete acceptance is what I need to be more focussed on. It would be wonderful if the governments current curriculum could make more room to explore this terribly under-rated option. Funnily enough all religions say 'know thyself', but they never seem to give any instructions. Knowing yourselves, being aware of yourselves in all situations, is the pathway to the love which is inside you all. I would like to be more involved with this.

ME All this seems to mean that at present we may be harming ourselves. There is so much fear in our society that we are continually focussed on having to defend ourselves.

EDUCATION Yes, you can see this can't you by the amount of devastating wars and other conflicts there are in your societies? Your prisons are bulging with people who have lost their way. Many people seem to be becoming more and more confused. You definitely need to shake me up a little, because at the moment you are often misusing me. I am mortified by this.

The thing is that you could be teaching your older children the art of self awareness, the investigation of themselves without judgement. To be able to teach this you need to first learn it for yourselves. Objective observation of yourselves in all your relationships is crucial. Very young children just need to be loved and accepted as they are.

The trouble is that children arrive in the world and they are immediately subject to all your beliefs and those of the society that they are born into. It's called conditioning, and different conditioning creates different cultures.

CONDITIONING That's right, I happen when you take on the beliefs of other people. I especially occur a lot when you are children and are learning about the world and how to be in it. Children are like sponges and tend to soak up the beliefs and ideas of their parents, their teachers, of the particular culture that they live in, their religions, their governments and so on. Children are particularly susceptible to me, they come into this world and are bombarded by me.

ME   So what is that going to do to them?

EDUCATION   It would be great if what they are being born into and bombarded by was all about love. But, as we have just seen it is not, it's often quite the opposite. When you have a strong belief in something, it tends to make you think this is the best way, and the others over there who don't have that particular belief, are wrong. It invites judgement of others, which tends to separate people. This judgement and sense of separation often causes conflict, which can then invite war. The threat of war invites fear and fear invites the need to defend yourselves.

Flags are symbols of separation. Added to this, there is another undercurrent of fear produced by the fact that everything is always changing. For most of you nothing feels secure or stable in this world. The temptation to have beliefs is strong, because beliefs make you feel more secure, they make you feel like you belong somewhere special, so you will be looked after. However, strong beliefs also lead to a closed mind, an unquestioning mind, because we think we 'know' it all already. The invitation is to move out of the beliefs and imagined security, and find your own way of being in the world.

CONDITIONING I agree. Having strong beliefs is what I am all about. The trouble is that I happen when you are not aware, you don't even realise I'm slipping in there. You think I'm a good thing because of that feeling of belonging I give you. Thus I seem to ward off the fear of being alone in an unreliable world. So I have lured you into my trap of judgement, fear and conflict.

ME Are you the reason there have been so many wars in the name of religion?

CONDITIONING Indeed I am. I am the perfect ingredient needed for starting a war. I'm right and you are wrong, so you both go charging off into battle. Of course there are other reasons such as territory, greed, money, etc but the thing is I'm getting fed up with all the drama, misery and craziness I am helping to cause.

ME So how do we get out of your trap?

EDUCATION That's where I can come in. You can get out of the trap by practicing the ways of self awareness. Question all your beliefs. Learn how to be still and aware. See very clearly the way you relate to other people, to yourself, to ideas, to nature and everything else in the world. By learning to notice and question everything you become more discerning and free. By noticing how you react to things, especially things that make you uncomfortable, you become more aware. Become an expert at noticing the feelings you have and where they appear as sensations in your body. These are some of the important things you can be teaching yourselves. Then when you are self aware enough, you will be able to teach it to the children.

It's also important to teach children how to read and write, and all the other things that they need to be able to do, to function efficiently in the world. But it's thousands of times more important to encourage them how to be self aware. With self awareness they become more open minded, more at home in the world and able to find their own passions, their own way, their own creativity, their own inspiration. Self awareness teaches them to rely on their own discernment and so not to accept all the beliefs that are showered upon them from people who think that they know best. It's not an accident that some of the most creative, inspired and inventive people in the world, failed miserably at school. Maybe it is something to do with the fact that they had an innate ability to think outside the box?

So can you please make sure that your box is transparent, flexible or preferably invisible, so that your view of life is infinitely enormous! If you are open-minded, your child's view of the world is more likely to be so too.

Which reminds me, in your teaching of history you seem to have conveniently fast forwarded over the first sixty thousand plus years of your existence on this planet, and said to yourselves 'nothing much happened there'. This is so not true. It is causing you such tunnel vision, it has not only made your view of the world to shrink, but has rendered you almost completely blind. You seem to have replaced those ancestors very sustainable way of life which lasted all that time, with what is turning out to be your extremely unsustainable, complicated way of life which is threatening to end in disaster.

Tribal life has much to teach you about how to live. It is especially teaming with examples of how to live side by side without too much reaction. Tribal life also shows how to respect the earth and how to respect each other. Peaceful ways of resolving difficulties were important to them. They could not move far away from their birth place, they could not run away. The lore that they lived by did not allow this and it taught them much.

In your present way of life there is very little guidance in moving from child to teenager, and from teenager to adult. In other words what is called 'rights of passage'. In tribal times it was a major part of a young persons life and education. The boys were put through great challenges. Thus they honed their courage. It was a way of honouring them at the same time as challenging them to step outside their comfort zone. The ceremonies would go on for several days or longer, and the whole tribe was involved in one way or another. The girls were honoured and celebrated as they passed from girlhood into womanhood. When they married they often had to leave their family home and move to the man's tribe. Being challenged is an important way of helping children to move through the changes of life, and without it all sorts of troubles arise. Rights of passage seems to be sadly neglected, not recognised enough in your present way of life.

As for self awareness, there are many ways of teaching it to children. Firstly be curious, ask them about themselves, how they feel, how they relate to things, ideas, people, animals and nature. And really listen to their answers. Find out what inspires them, what they love doing, what they find easy and what they find hard. Challenge them to step outside their comfort zone.

Ask them whether they can feel sensations in and on their body, and if so where do they feel them, and what do they feel like. Encourage them to be aware of themselves in different situations, especially when they experience difficult ones. Encourage them to take responsibility for their actions, but to be kind to themselves at the same time.

If a child is being difficult, rather than disciplining him, the teacher could question the child to find out what is going on. There are many exercises using drawing, music, and other forms of art that they can do to explore themselves and how they feel. Self knowledge is our return ticket to freedom, and freedom is not connected to any ideology or belief system.

Please reassess your view of me as quickly as you can because I need to be proud of what I do.

15

MANNERS and PARENTS

ME   So parents, what are you teaching your children in the way of manners?

PARENTS   That's easy, to be polite and civilised, so that they can live a respectable life.

ME   So Parents, what do you really think about that? I do wonder what is actually going on. I can see it's all very nice to be kind and polite and not hurt people's feelings, but doesn't that come at some expense? Are you denying their realness, their authenticity in some way? Do you think there might actually be a chance that you could be teaching your children to lie? Could there be some truth in that?

PARENTS   Oh my God, we never thought of it like that. That's actually a bit of a shock!

MANNERS   Well the danger is if you don't use us, you can really offend people, and then they won't like you.

ME   Maybe, but whose responsibility is it whether people get offended?

MANNERS   Well it's ours I suppose.

ME   Really, is it really? Surely not in a world where everyone is taking responsibility for how they feel?

PARENTS   But not everyone is taking responsibility for how they feel, and then they get upset, so what do we do about that?

ME   Leave them to it. You can't force them to take responsibility. Can't you see that if we all took responsibility then all would be well in the world?

PARENTS   I suppose so, and if that is the case, then the only people that we can get to be responsible are ourselves. What a relief!

ME   That's right. You don't have to make them be responsible, that's up to them. And remember, if you teach children to pretend, then you are not teaching them to be authentic. Which do you think is more important, being truthful and authentic, or being untruthful and pretentious? Supposing your child upsets someone and you force them to go and apologise, and they don't want to because they don't feel sorry. Surely you are making them do something that feels false to them? You are teaching them to lie, to be inauthentic.

PARENTS   Yes we can see that now, but what do you suggest that we do?

ME   Well it might be a good idea to stop and have a conversation with them about whatever is going on, whatever 'problem' the child is having. Ask questions. Listen carefully to their answers. So often we forget to ask questions or listen to their answers. Inquire what is going on for the child. Be curious. Ask and find out. Explore the stories. Get them into their feelings. Encourage awareness rather than jump in and tell then to 'be polite.'

MANNERS   Can't you have us as well as authenticity?

ME   Yes Manners, you can, in an ideal world. If you encourage children to be authentic they will be more likely to be happy and treat others well. This is because they know themselves better, and so are bursting with love. Just be aware that in a not so ideal world, people may be confused and not taking responsibility. They may feel like they can't be truthful, they have to be 'nice' so as not to hurt anyone. Then it could be at the expense of authenticity.

MANNERS   Actually we can see we would be unnecessary in a very aware world, where everyone is taking responsibility for how they feel, and therefore not blaming anyone else.

PARENTS   Yes that's true isn't it Manners? Having you in our lives does make it easier to live with people, but it means we sometimes tiptoe around each other, pretending, and not saying what we really feel, and also not really looking into ourselves with honesty. Consequently, we do not encourage our children to do so either, which is very sad and unhelpful. We have to learn how to discern whether it comes from our hearts, or whether we are only saying it because we were taught to be nice. This is crucial to becoming authentic. Authenticity only comes from the heart. Taking responsibility is a way to the heart.

16

PERPETRATOR, VICTIM and RESCUER

ME   When I was at lifeline doing the training to be on the telephones, we did an exercise with you three.

PERPETRATOR, VICTIM, RESCUER   (all looking alarmed)......Really, oh dear.

ME   Yes, and we had to act it out, so let's have a go now and see what happens. Miss Perpetrator, you usually start these incidents, so if you could start doing your thing now, we'll see what happens.

PERPETRATOR   (looking reluctant)

ME   Go on then,

PERPETRATOR   (loud, screaming).....I   want   my dessert....(more screaming)

VICTIM   (soft voice) No Darling, I love you very much but you can't have dessert until you've eaten your veggies.

PERPETRATOR   (screaming louder, louder, louder)

VICTIM   (pleading voice) Please Darling, that's not very nice.

PERPETRATOR (more screaming) I need it now, you're being mean to me.

VICTIM (wimpy, sad, powerless, voice), That's not a nice way to speak to me.

PERPETRATOR (more loud screaming)

RESCUER OK Perpetrator, (picking her up with authority and carrying her outside) that's enough of that, you need to calm down.

ME Now think about it, is that a happy way to live? The interesting thing is, you all have favourite roles you can sometimes swap around. For instance if the original Rescuer gets fed up enough, he/she may become angry and become the Perpetrator by attacking the original perpetrator, who becomes the Victim. And the original Victim tries to make it all right and becomes the Rescuer. Alternatively, there might be times when the original Rescuer and Victim start having a go at each other, then the original Perpetrator tries to sort it out thus becoming the Rescuer. It's really all a big drama involving massive amounts of stress and upset, probably stemming from some unresolved issues.

VICTIM It is a big drama isn't it? If I get pushed hard enough I can easily become the Perpetrator, but that feels terrible, so I choose to remain the victim.

PERPETRATOR and RESCUER Yes we can see that too, but it all seems very real to us. We seem to be caught in it, we're in a trap. Is there a way out?

ME   There's always a way out, you just have to find it.

PERPETRATOR, VICTIM, RESCUER   Really, but how?

ME   Well Victim, the skill is in saying NO with so much authenticity, so much strength, so much calmness, so little agitation or anger, that the Perpetrator believes you. If there's a trace of uncertainty, fear or anger the Perpetrator will feel it and not believe you. You have to know exactly what you want and stick to it.

PERPETRATOR, VICTIM, RESCUER   So the bottom line is authenticity is it? If everyone is being authentic and not playing their roles, then we will be annihilated.

ME   I guess so, but what if just one of you stopped playing their roll and opted out of it completely, what would happen then?

PERPETRATOR, VICTIM   Well if Rescuer stopped playing, we two would be left to fight it out, or rather Perpetrator would bully Victim out of his mind, because there would be no-one there to rescue her/him. Though I have a sneaky feeling you are going to tell us what Victim can do.

ME   That's right, Victim how do you think you stop a bully.

VICTIM   (looking blank and shrugging.)

ME   Tell me, have you ever tried not reacting?

VICTIM   (In a small but curious voice.) No.

ME   Well I suggest you try it.

PERPETRATOR   (Looking a bit worried) Yes that would be something different. My power would be all gone, whoosh, out the window.

VICTIM   The trouble is I feel powerless and I don't know if I could be strong enough to not react.

ME   It might help if you became more aware of why you react. Do you remember earlier I mentioned unresolved issues? Really they are false beliefs and we all, or most of us anyway, have them, and they are often born in childhood. It's a good idea to start with ourselves, I don't know if you realise, but we can't change anyone else, only ourselves.

So think back to your childhood and do some enquiry. Some useful questions might be,

1. What was happening in your home?
2. When did it all begin?
3. What did you witness?
4. How did you react?
5. How did you cope?
6. What feelings did you have?
7. How did you treat the other family members?
8. How did you treat yourself?

I personally found the Byron Katie Work extremely helpful for, not only looking closely at my beliefs but very importantly, for turning them all around. This led me to getting to know myself better. It's such a gift, and a profound relief, to see the truth about ourselves and what's happening in our life, uncomfortable sometimes, but worth it to receive the gift.

VICTIM   I would like to be able to stop reacting, I can see that that would be amazing. Maybe I should give it a go.

ME   By the way, do you know what the difference between a Rescuer and a Peace-maker is?

PERSECUTOR, VICTIM, RESCUER   (looking perplexed but interested). No. Tell us please, something is telling us that we all need to know.

ME   A Peacemaker knows that that's exactly where the Perpetrator and Victim need to be because of their past experiences. Whereas a rescuer thinks there's something wrong with them both and their situation. Therefore the energy behind a Peacemaker is quite different from the energy behind a Rescuer. A Peacemaker is accepting, unattached to outcome and loving, whereas a Rescuer is judgemental, and somewhat desperate for change.

PERPETRATOR, VICTIM, RESCUER   Wow, if we do the work on ourselves, we will all be annihilated and then we can go on to being more useful, more authentic and more loving.

ME   Yep, that's the truth. Happy enquiring.

17

MISTAKES and ACCIDENTS

ME   Hello Mistake, what are you really?

MISTAKE   My name says it all really, I am a Miss Take. Every happening, event or moment in life is a 'take'. Like in the movies when they're trying to film a particular scene they say take one, take two, take three etc. until they get it right. So it is in life. Every moment is just another shot at whatever is going on, and if it doesn't work out 'right' you call it a mistake, which is me.

ME   In other words, you are the choice that leads to an uncomfortable result for me.

MISTAKE   That's right. I usually bring up some quite powerful emotions for you. You think of me as a bad thing, when really I am in fact more of an opportunity. An opportunity for some kind of learning, quite often a learning in the forgiveness department, and usually forgiveness of yourself.

The emotions I bring up for you are wide and varied, ranging from embarrassment and regret, to fear and anger. Sometimes I can be extremely large and devastating, and other times I can be a little hiccup in the scheme of things. Whichever I am, remember I am not bad, but an opportunity for self discovery. I have a cousin called Accident who is similar to me, though he will probably argue black and blue he is nothing like me. Are you there Accident?

ACCIDENT I most certainly am and you're right I am nothing like you. If you look me up in the dictionary you will see the proof of this, I have a different meaning entirely to you. The dictionary says that I am 'an event without apparent cause, something that happens by chance'. Whereas for you it says 'error or fault in thought or action'. So that means that you are guilty, whereas I am not.

MISTAKE That's because people are so unwilling to take responsibility, so I think you should go and talk to responsibility before you decide you are completely blameless. Anyway we are both food for realisations and learning.

ME Who wrote the dictionary anyway?

18

GUILT

ME   I have been puzzling as to whether you are a feeling or not?

GUILT   No, I am not a feeling. I am actually a state of mind, and I am born by thought. I am really a story that you believe. If you look closely you will find that hiding behind me, keeping very quiet, is a feeling. Quieten your mind and look carefully, closely to see if you can catch a glimpse of the feeling. Ask yourself what the feeling is that lobbed you into the situation.

ME   But what if it's an accident?

GUILT   Look deeper, deeper, deeper. What was going on the moment before the accident? What were you thinking about? What were you doing? What were you conscious of or unconscious of? How present were you? Where was your mind? What was your mind saying? What were you telling yourself?Answer those questions and the feeling will most probably rear its head. Once you have seen the feeling, you are in the the field of forgiveness. The only way to rise above it is to own the feeling, which requires courage and the ability to become vulnerable, vulnerable enough to forgive yourself.

ME And what if there is another person involved?

GUILT Well then it's their turn to go on a journey, the journey within, the journey to forgiveness.

ME Forgiveness is a beautiful thing.

GUILT He is a wonderful friend.

19

BALANCE

ME OK Balance, explain please, what are you all about?

BALANCE Well, I am the ultimate state. You live in a world of duality or opposites and I am the trick, the joker, the ideal state, I am the point of ascension. When I arrive in your life you will be surprised, but the surprise is a secret so I can't tell you, that wouldn't be any good for you at all. You have to find me, find the balance, find out for yourselves. When you have found me, certain things will drop away, or maybe the certain things have to drop away and then you will find me.

ME So how do we find out?

BALANCE Ask Awareness, she will help you. I am all about action, so remember to take action if needed when you have noticed an imbalance, that's the hard bit sometimes. Mostly all the action needed is just to notice, to observe, to be aware.

20

PAIN and SUFFERING

ME   Hi you two, I recently heard a saying that goes, 'life happens for us, not to us'. So if that's true, can you please explain exactly what on earth are you doing in our lives? Why can't you leave us alone to get on with it? Why do you have to keep butting in and upsetting everything?

PAIN and SUFFERING   You should know, after all it's you that lets us in, you're the one reacting, but actually if you're questioning whether life happens for you and not to you, the light must be beginning to dawn. Life is after all a gift, and things are maybe not the way you thought they were.

ME   Yes, you're quite right, I have been thinking for quite a while now, 'What if all the bad circumstances we sometimes find ourselves in could in some way be for our benefit? In fact, I remember now, of course the bad things that happen are there for us and not to us because the worst thing that ever happened to me and made me suicidal at the time, turned out to be the best thing after all. It took a while for me to realise this, and while I was going through the grieving thing you were there a lot. But when I'd got through it, I could see things entirely differently, and I was so grateful for the experience. Mind you, it does seem to be unbearable when you are right in the thick of it. The thing is life must happen for us because if it didn't it would all be a bit pointless wouldn't it?

PAIN and SUFFERING   That's right, so why do you think we're here? Wouldn't it be something to do with the fact that you are in a world of duality, right wrong, good bad, pain pleasure, suffering enjoyment etc etc. You can't have one without the other, so here we are. The only way you can have both and be at peace is if you are in perfect balance, and then you ascend anyway. So I guess really you want to know how to be in perfect balance, do you follow us?

ME   Yes, so how do I do that?

PAIN and SUFFERING   Ask him and see if he replies.

ME   Ask who?

PAIN and SUFFERING   Balance. Or you could ask Awareness he is all about evenness of mind. Learning how to not react is the important thing. To feel me and at the same time to have a calm, even mind.

ME   A mind that's in balance?

PAIN and SUFFERING   Yes, absolutely. Not a particularly easy thing to do, but well worth it if you persevere.

21

JUDGEMENT and ACCEPTANCE

ME Oh there you are again Judgement, you seem to be popping in a lot lately.

JUDGEMENT I do seem to be, don't I? I wonder why that is? Could it possibly be that you are all just too keen on me. It might be a good idea to take a minute and see if you can catch a glimpse of the misery you are inadvertently wading around in because of your misguided use of me.

ME Indeed I can, and I feel more and more of us are realising how detrimental you are to our state of mind. The trouble is, you are just very easy to lob into. It's become a real habit. And when something so called "bad" happens you seem to be the one we call on. I can see that the world would be a much happier place if you weren't quite so popular with us.

JUDGEMENT The thing is you don't question yourselves enough, and you have some very set beliefs which are a bit dubious and could do with a strong spotlight to make them less shadowy. A bit more curiosity and questioning would go a long way to getting rid of me! The use of shoulds and shouldn'ts are a good way of spotting me, as are right's, wrong's, good's and bad's etc. Notice if you are using me against yourself.

I do have a good use though. For instance I am very good at helping you to know when it's safe to cross the road. I am called in a lot for things like that, and that's what I am really for, but I can see you have allowed yourselves to over use me far too much in some very inappropriate ways.

ME   Actually I can see when we use you indiscriminately you are really very separating.

JUDGEMENT   Yes I have to admit I am. But it's up to you to become aware. First of all, notice I seem to go hand in hand with beliefs. The moment you have a set of strong beliefs about something, it means that I have been utilised, and quite often, through no fault of my own, I can back-fire on you. Questioning your beliefs can be very interesting because they may not be serving you as well as you think. Actually they may be separating you from other people, which can cause you a lot of agitation and heartache. I'm not saying anything more, because it's up to you to persevere if you want to be a bit clearer about the predicament you have got yourselves into with me. And remember, Acceptance is my antidote.

ACCEPTANCE   Oh my goodness, I was wondering how long it would take! All that preamble, but you finally got there. What a relief.

ME   It sure is isn't it? To find you is very liberating.

ACCEPTANCE   I pretty much solve everything don't I?

ME   Yes, you are like the perfume of a flower on a hot summers night, wafting in to make everything perfect.

ACCEPTANCE That's right, I am the balm on the wound, the fragrance of freedom, the perfume of peace. However, don't use me without discernment. If you have got yourself into a situation which you don't like and feel trapped, maybe it's time to take action rather than sit in it and suffer. The decision is yours, remember you have to look after yourself and treat yourself kindly.

22

VIRTUE

VIRTUE   I am not earned by being 'good' or doing the 'right' thing you know. A lot of people think this. Some people try to cultivate me, and if that's the case it probably isn't really me. I am not attained by trying to be something you're not.

ME   I always used to think that was the case. I was trapped in the good girl syndrome for so long. I see now it wasn't authentic, because it sprang out of fear, fear of not being loved. Authenticity comes from truth, the truth of the moment. This seems to mean that anyone can be infused with you, is that right?

VIRTUE   Yes of course, absolutely. I arise when you recognise your so called faults, the things you are not so proud of about yourself. Recognise them with no sense of wanting to change them. Notice them passively with no judgement.

It doesn't matter how bad you think they are, that's just your judgement. I arise when you look them straight in the eye. I arise when you make friends with them, acknowledge and accept them so completely, so intensely, with no sense of wanting to change them, that freedom from them eventually arises. Love, joy, peace, freedom and me emerge from the slurry. This is truly the miracle of alchemy.

23

SUICIDE

ME   You are such an extreme action, people think you are a way out of this life, but are you really?

SUICIDE   No, no, no, no. no. I am an avoidance, probably of something uncomfortable. The trouble with thinking it's a way out, is that everything we don't face and deal with will come back to haunt us next time round. If you use me, you miss the magic of discovering something new and different about yourself and your life. But you have to be prepared to stick with the problem and find the courage to ask yourselves enough questions, to go within and sit in the feeling. It's important to get help if you are struggling. Remember, one moment follows another. It's no different at death; birth always follows on its heals, so there you are again, with the same old miserable 'problem', though it may look different. So if you kill yourself because you can't stand the situation that you are in, low and behold it'll come back in your next lifetime to bite you in the butt. Lovely to think we could escape that easily but if we could, there would be nothing to learn and life would have no meaning.

ME   How can you say that, life will have no meaning?

SUICIDE Well if we're here to get to know ourselves, remember all religions say know thyself, then surely we'd be given another chance? It's not going to necessarily all happen in one life-time. And do you think that someone who uses me knows themselves?

ME What do you mean?

SUICIDE What emotions would you think someone is having who is thinking about ending it all?

ME I think he'd be full of pain and suffering, either physical or emotional. He would be unhappy in some way, desperate, fed up with life for some reason, sad, and a whole host of other negative emotions.

SUICIDE So he definitely wouldn't be feeling peaceful, happy, fulfilled, abundant, loving and free would he?

ME No, it doesn't seem that way to me. There would be some very big negative stories and feelings overwhelming him. Stories and feelings which he didn't want to deal with; judgements either against himself or others. Otherwise there would be no point in taking such an action. So it seems as if he would be trying to escape something which is important, and something which is not only important but which is essential for his awareness and understanding of life.

SUICIDE Yes, whenever you face a difficult situation and deal with it, life opens up a bit more. Afterwards you find you have more understanding. It's very important to face death with equanimity and as much peace as you can generate. I wish everyone would hurry up and realise this, so I can retire from this awfully negative occupation. Remember people, everything is forgivable and nobody is bad or evil. We all make mistakes. Be willing to look, and go on looking, and go on looking, and all will be well.

24

THE BYRON KATIE WORK

ME You know when I first heard about you I knew I had to try you out.

THE BYRON KATIE WORK What did you think?

ME I was both amazed and shocked. I was amazed because you took me and showed me that many of my beliefs weren't as rock solid true as I thought they were. I was shocked because some of them seemed to be more true about myself than the other person! Either way the scales fell from my eyes leaving me feeling much freer and clearer. I could see those beliefs made the prison that they actually were, separating me from other people. They were also stopping me from knowing myself truthfully.

THE BYRON KATIE WORK I'm just four questions and what I call a 'turnaround', but when you apply them to yourself I can blast through those beliefs like a bolt of lightening, can't I?

ME You certainly can. The first belief I used you on was 'My son shouldn't drink so much alcohol'. He was far too keen on it in my opinion, and I had a lot of stories and beliefs about why this was true. For example, 'my son will damage himself if he keeps drinking so much'. As I focussed on each of the six beliefs that I had concerning my son's drinking habits, and worked through your list of questions followed by the 'turnaround' on each one, a whole new view of life dropped into my awareness. My son shouldn't drink so much alcohol became, my son should drink so much alcohol, (because that's what he does). My son will damage himself if he keeps drinking so much alcohol became I will damage myself if I keep (worrying about him) drinking so much alcohol! I found that when you stop arguing with what's actually happening, peace arises. Much to my amazement I became peaceful with the fact that my son kept consuming enormous quantities of alcohol. My relationship with him (and with myself), improved dramatically. All my worrying turned out to be a waste of time, and was helping neither of us!

THE BYROM KATIE WORK   It sounds like you had a bit of an epiphany.

ME   Oh yes, a rather large epiphany actually, it woke me up big time. I stopped feeling responsible for his behaviour, and crept back into my own business! It's hard to keep out of someone else's business until you realise how damaging it is for you both. It's hard to trust someone when you have unhelpful beliefs about them.

Afterwards I utilised you frequently for a long time. It was confronting at first, but as my view of life unravelled, it became easier and easier. It seemed as though I was viewing some major parts of my life back to front in some way!

Be prepared to be truthful though, The Byron Katie Work is not about being nice, kind and spiritual! It's about finding the truth about yourself. So leap right in, guns blazing, be as nit-picky as you like, and tell it as it is.

THE BYRON KATIE WORK   That's what I'm for, blast away the cobwebs, free yourself up, and get in touch with the authentic you.

Do you still use me?

ME   Whenever I spot that I'm having a judgement about anything or anyone; a friend, a neighbour, a relation, a corporation, myself, a government, even my body, my eyesight or anything else in my life, there you are, available as always.

25

STARS

ME   Hey you shiny wee glittery things winking down from on high with the ultimate bird's eye view, what do you see?

STARS   What are you guys trying to do? Block us out completely? Why?

We are so beautiful, we may be far away but what a picture we make, why do you want to obliterate us?

All those fumes and lights obscuring us from your view. You're going to forget us soon and that makes us very sad. Our hearts are breaking.

No wonder you're having so many floods, storms, droughts devastating fires and earthquakes etc. You cannot keep doing ignorant things in the name of 'progress' and greed without severe consequences.

Soon you won't know where you're going, 'cos we will not twinkle so, and you'll be lost in all the trappings of desire and craving. Wake up now, people, and see what you are doing. Open your hearts and find the love for us and each other. No one is exempt.

Look up and see the vastness, and the mystery of it all. Ask yourselves 'where does it end?' Rest in that question for a while without expecting an answer. Of course, if you think you don't need us because you are so clever and you can do it all on your own, just be careful, be very, very careful my friends. A little cleverness goes a long way, please add some Wisdom. It may pay you handsomely to take your eyes off your screens for a minute and gaze up at the display above you, and to celebrate us for the messages we shower upon you.

We do notice you can't even sit and wait for half an hour without absentmindedly reaching for your latest device. And that you spend an awful lot of time indoors, especially at night, so some of you are maybe completely oblivious of us. We are constant and reliable, because we change so slowly compared to things on earth. We are a source to be depended on. We implore you.....tune into our frequency.....drink in the heavens......bask at night under our glittering majesty.....learn to read us like the first people did. And celebrate.

ME   Wow, that's quite a dressing down you just gave me. The trouble is everything is changing so fast it seems that you could be a little out of date.

STARS   Not if you know how to observe. It's true things do change all the time, but that's just a part of it. Most importantly observe yourselves, and then observe nature. No matter how many inventions you make, do not forget your humble beginnings. Observe yourselves first and you will then know all you need to know. Notice the changes.

Record them and go from there. Remember how the skies cleared above polluted cities when covid was on and you couldn't drive anywhere? Things will change if you allow it. Remember the important things folks, record them before you forget.

26

WORRY, ANXIETY, SECURITY, INSECURITY and CHANGE

ME   Hello Worry, Hello Anxiety, You're both here again, I can feel you, in my stomach and in my head…..

WORRY   Oh I know, you're calling me in a lot lately and I'm so tired. The trouble is you're far too friendly with me, and I'm getting a bit fed up with it, cos I could do with a few weeks off really……

ANXIETY   Yes me too, my god it's extremely exhausting for us both. I wish you'd stop.

ME   I'm really sorry but I can't seem to help it. I think the main trouble is that Security is always vanishing just when I need him most. I just get something all sorted and then something else changes and Security flies out the window, and you both move right in. You think it's exhausting for you, you should have a go at being me.

WORRY, ANXIETY   The question is this, 'Are you going to make that Security fellow stay forever?' It seems to me the more you see him the more you want him …..so you're never satisfied, you haven't really grasped the fact that nothing stays the same in this world, everything is always changing and that's the way it's meant to be.

CHANGE Ah ha, you've all seen me now, and I'm the one behind it all it seems. I'm the one that makes both of you; I apparently create you Security, and also your not so popular brother Insecurity. You think you would like everything to stay the same. You think that everything has to be rosy, rosy, rosy I suppose. Unfortunately you live in a world of duality, and that just ain't going to happen because of me..... oh dear. Your peaceful little haven is a bit more precarious than you would like, but I do have an antidote.

ME Oh so it's you Change, you tricky little devil, always coming along when I think I've got things sorted.....what's the antidote?

CHANGE Well, what makes you feel so insecure?

ME Well, I think that underneath it all is the fact that maybe I'm going to suddenly find myself without any money, and then I wouldn't be able to buy any food, and then I'd be hungry.

CHANGE Ah, so you're allowing your mind to zoom off into the future eh? Might be a good idea to stay in the present, don't you think?

SECURITY The trick is this...........(long pause)

ME, WORRY, ANXIETY Go on then, put us out of our misery......

SECURITY Well…..The thing is, like Change says, you can't have one of us without the other. He is intent on making everything in this world change constantly, so nothing stays the same. Therefore, like it or not, there is indeed another side of me called Insecurity and so if you're going to live peacefully with us all, you need to love all three of us. It would be so wonderful for you. Just imagine the excitement of falling in love with Change and Insecurity as well as me. What a roller coaster….. but such a joyous one.

CHANGE I'm glad you included me in all this because after all, like you said, I am the Master, the one behind it all…..

ME Yes, but how do I fall in love with Insecurity? Security yes, that is comfortable, but Insecurity, that's a very uncomfortable proposition, and as for you Change….. well…..

INSECURITY Huh, thanks for mentioning me in such a derogatory way, I'm only uncomfortable because you can't handle me properly…..

SECURITY (Giving Insecurity a withering look). Well try observing us properly then, both of us…..just observe and savour us…..stop judging both of us. There probably is a grain of truth to the thought that you aren't handling Insecurity properly. And maybe it would be a good idea to stop thinking of me as a flighty problem. Instead, just notice us both when we come to call, as well as our Master CHANGE. Allow us all some space, allow us all to be there, and feel us all in your body, that amazingly intelligent vehicle you inhabit. Remember though, the number one rule, no judgement of us at all, that is very important. And like Change said earlier, staying in the present moment is important. If you trust your body more, it will show you the way. Relish and savour all three of us, fall in love with us and you may find that you will be a lot happier.

CHANGE   Well done Security, fall in love with us all, that is indeed the antidote.

27

CRAVING and AVERSION

ME   Hello there you two, how are you both doing?

CRAVING and AVERSION   Well we're still here alive and well, thanks, and having a lot of fun with you all.

ME   I need you to explain yourselves so that I can do something about you. I know you probably want to be on your way. Could you please tell me why you're still hanging around.

CRAVING and AVERSION   Not sure we really want to be on our way that much. Like we said, watching the drama is quite fun, but it's also quite sad. So we just thought a little more explanation would help you.

ME   Right. Well that's good. I would love to know what you have to say for yourselves.

CRAVING   Oh please let me go first, I'm dying to make him understand us more.

AVERSION   Oh OK, if you must.

CRAVING   I come into your life when you judge something as so pleasant that you want it again and again and again. However, it's not necessarily the experience that you want, but the pleasant sensations that that experience engenders within you. These sensations are felt as vibrations in the body, feel good sensations. I'll give you an example. You're sitting at home, watching a movie, when a sense of something missing arises, a feeling of emptiness. You think to yourself, ummmm something sweet would be nice.

You go to the fridge, and low and behold there's a whole stock of things just waiting for this slightly empty occasion. Which should I choose? You decide on one and then go back to the movie. The taste was marvellous. I'll have another. Before you know it you've emptied the fridge.

The again and again bit, that's me. That's when I've got you in my evil grip. You're using me big time.

ME What if it's a drug?

CRAVING Same thing. It's not the actual drug that you want. It's the sensation that it produces in your body. That is what is so attractive, it draws you in again and again. And guess what? I'm right there.

ME So is it the same with everything that we want to do again and again?

CRAVING Not necessarily. It depends how much you'd miss it, how compulsive it is. If your world falls apart if you can't do it, or if you have no control over it, then it's me. It's important to be discerning about how the thing you're doing is affecting you, and therefore whether you're doing it for the wrong reason. Take exercise for instance, which we all know is a good thing to do. If you do it a lot it produces a thing called dopamine in your body, and dopamine makes you feel good. If you're doing it to get the high, then maybe it's me. The other thing that is important to notice is how something is affecting the other people and activities in your life. Notice whether you are neglecting others, or something you have to get done, because of what you are doing.

ME Is there a feeling going on when we're using you?

CRAVING Yes there certainly is, and it's different in each case for everyone. With the above example it was a feeling of emptiness while watching the movie, but it could be loneliness or boredom or any one of a hundred other feelings. That's for you to notice.

AVERSION Hello everyone, Can I have my turn now… ask me why I'm here.

ME OK Aversion, tell us why are you here.

AVERSION Well let's suppose that something happens to you and it makes you feel uncomfortable, and you then judge it to be bad. I'll give you a few examples.

- You get married, things go pear-shaped and you get divorced.
- You make a speech at your friends wedding and the jokes all fall flat.

- You take a risk on the stock market and loose all your money.
- You taste a piece of paw paw, it's a bit over-ripe, so you spit it out.

Afterwards, if the opportunity to do any of those things again enters your life, you possibly might decide not to do it again. You don't want to feel those uncomfortable sensations that you felt when it all went wrong, ever again. Those uncomfortable sensations can be any one of a whole smorgasbord of reactions such as fear, embarrassment, disgust, depression, hopelessness, blah blah blah. So you make the decision, I'm certainly not doing that again.

Well my friend I'm afraid I've got you in my grip, I have control over you. So you keep yourself safe by not going there ever again. You limit your life, and effectively, you are living in the past, through a past reaction. You are my prisoner.

ME   Ouch, that is so sad.

AVERSION   It certainly is. So whenever you feel uncomfortable about doing something, just know that there is a challenge awaiting you there, and you may like to take positive action on it. The thing is that life is all about balance. I am on one end of the scale and Craving is on the other end of the scale. The trick for you humans is to be able to stay in the middle, in the present moment. The trick is to stop dropping into the past or the future.

ME   That sounds fairly boring to me, I mean if we sat in the middle all the time we'd be a bit stuck wouldn't we?

CRAVING and AVERSION Oh no, heavens no…..That is the spot where you become still. Where you're living in the present and you ascend. The spot where you rise up, spread your wings and let go. I know it may not be easy for you to do because you have become so indoctrinated with reactions, fears, and addictions. Even though it's fun watching the drama, we would both really like to retire now. So, for heavens sake next time you feel either of us entering your field of experience, do us a favour. Be still. Become aware. Balance yourself. Find that spot, that wider view, the bigger picture, the inspired action. Grab the moment and fly like an eagle soaring upwards into the thermal of life.

ME I can see how you are both distracting me from living fully. The question is, how do I get in the middle and be still so that I can banish you both?

CRAVING and AVERSION Awareness mate, that's what you need. Also a little courage, daring, curiosity and willingness would help.

CRAVING I'd just like to say that I'm a lot harder to spot than Aversion, just so you know.

ME What do you mean?

CRAVING Remember that bit about having a wee bit of me for things that are actually good for you? Well it's still me. I'm still there. Which means that you are not really free. Even sitting somewhere in meditation, I can still creep in when you aren't aware. Usually I bring with me my friend Desperation, who makes you feel a little bit more hyped up about it, like you really, really, really need to get better at it or something. So beware of the wanting. It's always a sign of a feeling of lack. Be aware my friend, super aware, otherwise it may all back-fire on you.

ME   So how do I get more Awareness?

CRAVING and AVERSION   Go and ask him, Awareness that is, he's ever so helpful and friendly.

28

MEDITATION

ME When I drove down the road to the Meditation centre where I first met you, I had the distinct feeling that I was coming home. This seemed odd at the time as I had never been interested in you before. The only thing I did know was that I had to learn how to still my mind, because it was driving me absolutely crazy. As soon as I heard about you; (the meditation with the strange name), I suspected that you were going to be the way out of my misery. So there I was, driving through the puddles into the Vipassana Meditation Centre.

VIPASSANA MEDITATION Suddenly there I was in your life.....what a relief eh!

ME Yes it certainly was because I seem to have an extremely busy mind!

VIPASSANA MEDITATION Well then, you had certainly arrived at the right place. Body and mind are intimately linked, but mind is tricky and leads you on many a wild goose chase, detouring all over the place. Consequently you mostly stay trapped in either the past or the future. Mind does not want you to be in the present moment. Body however, will unswervingly show you the truth about yourself. I am a technique which works with body sensations, and any meditation that does this will help you to know yourself.

ME Yes, I see that now, but at the time I had very little idea that I needed to get to 'know myself'.

The first three days of the course were spent taming that unruly mind of mine. I noticed that it kept luring me away from the practice. As the first three days passed I gradually, with a great amount of difficulty, became more focussed. During the remaining seven days I was taught how to use my slightly calmer mind to examine the sensations in my body.

VIPASSANA MEDITATION I am not a religion. I do not tell people what to believe. The body holds all the habit patterns of the mind as sensations. I am a way of observing those sensations objectively with no judgement either good or bad. The centres where I am taught provide a space in which to do this. You are free to come to your own realisations.

ME You are a gift which I was in desperate need of, and I am so grateful you came into my life.

29

BOREDOM, AGITATION and ADDICTION

ME   Hello you three, I never realised before that you are such good friends.

BOREDOM, AGITATION, ADDICTION   We are, and we sometimes work together, and boy are we successful in the present world situation.

ME   Agitation, you are so familiar it's taken me a long time to recognise you, because I actually thought you were a part of me, and that that's the way it should, and always would be. You were there when I was a baby crying for my mother. You were there when I was a young child immersed in painful confusion. You were there when I was a schoolgirl watching the clock in nearly every boring lesson. You were there every time I stepped out of my comfort zone which was at times a great deal. And you were there when I was unknowingly honing the misguided skills of fear and worrying. You were there at every single Vipassana Meditation course I have ever been to, which is where I finally realised that you are not me, you are an imposter. I could feel you vibrating throughout my body. A discordant note in every cell, you are merciless.

AGITATION   Well spotted, I am indeed an imposter, one that you allowed into your temple, but you've caught me now haven't you, even though it took you a while? Your nail-biting was a distraction wasn't it, at least you thought so for many years, but it didn't annihilate me, so I always sidled back in when you weren't aware. You needed me to give you a push into becoming more alert didn't you? I'm not always there now though am I? You've seen me now. Make sure you stay vigilant though, because you need to catch me every time I try to sneak back in! You know how crazily persistent I can be!

ME   I do, your persistence is exasperating, and quite often my vigilance slips, mostly when I am not busy enough. I seem to have this terrible need to keep busy which probably stems from the belief that its wrong to do nothing. I acquired this belief in my childhood when I consistently heard my mother admonishing my father for not doing enough. I notice that when I am not busy I am often not fully relaxed and in you come, spikes and all. I need to remember to consciously relax when I am not busy. I know I have to keep remembering because I can see that to be aware at all times is one of the most important things we can do in life.

AGITATION   Yes, and when you are aware all the time I will be out of a job. There are however an awful lot of you actually, so I have a feeling that I may not have to worry about that just yet!

ME   Tell me how you work with Boredom and Addiction.

AGITATION   Go on Boredom, enlighten her.

BOREDOM   I am usually the instigator, I slip in there when there's nothing much going on, when things are quiet, when there are no distractions. I am often felt in times of solitude. It's hard to catch me nowadays because there are so many distractions to take you away from me in this modern world.

ME   There are, aren't there.

BOREDOM   Yes, nowadays as soon as people feel me approaching they block me out. They pull out their phones or those computers with streams of continuous information. Podcasts, and social media with all that endless chit chat. And then there's the games, sometimes quite violent, dulling the mind. All of these devices are distancing people from taking part in life, from actually living, from relating with each other and life in general, and most importantly from feeling me.

ME   Why is it so important for them to feel you?

BOREDOM   Because I am a challenge. When people feel me I offer them the opportunity to be present with me, to relax and just be with me, to get to know me, and funnily enough if they can do this, and I admit that it is a challenge, it often leads them to creativity and inspiration. If they don't take up my challenge however, the challenge of hanging out with me, Agitation or Addiction, will most probably drop by, and the opportunity will be lost.

ME   So you start it all, then Agitation walks in closely followed by Addiction.

BOREDOM   I don't always start it, but sometimes I do. Addiction is your go to remedy, well you think he is but actually he is the ultimate trap. When you reach for your phone, your computer or the television, overindulge on food or drink, take drugs, or whatever else you choose to soothe or occupy your troubled self with, there you are in the arms of Addiction.

ME Hello Addiction. I didn't realise my nail-biting was you until recently, but I feel it is.

ADDICTION Yes that is right, anything that you have little or no control over so that it disrupts your life is me. Even though you may argue that it doesn't disrupt your life that much, it's no good excusing it and pretending it doesn't have any effect at all because if you are being honest you will see that it does, even if it just means that your nails look like crap. It's hard to admit sometimes that I am visiting you, isn't it?

ME Whoah, that's knocked me well and truly off my perch.

ADDICTION So let's go into it a bit deeper shall we. Are you ready?

ME Go on then, take me down.

ADDICTION You realise that you're not actually addicted to a substance or an action, but something else entirely don't you?

ME What do you mean?

ADDICTION You're using me to get a particular sensation. What is the sensation that you are seeking when you are biting your nails? Shut your eyes and go into it.

ME (closing my eyes). This is difficult. There is something satisfying about biting my nails, weird eh, it takes me away from the onslaught of the world, and gives me a moment of 'peace'. It's a moment of escape into myself. Maybe that's the sensation that I am seeking.... peace. It seems that there is nothing wrong with the sensation that I am seeking.

Biting my nails has become such a compulsive habit, sometimes I don't even realise that I am doing it. When I do catch myself doing it, I find it very difficult to stop and consciously allow my arms to relax. I have noticed lately though that allowing my arms to relax is actually quite a lovely feeling, and is all I really have to do. It's taken me such a long time to figure this out! Sixty eight years to be precise! I thought it was wrong to do nothing and relax, because that was what my father was so good at, and I was determined not to be like him at any cost! How crazy to be in such a rediculous but compelling trap.

ADDICTION and AGITATION   Yes, that sounds like us.

ME   It's a sorry state of affairs, because when we are allowing you into our lives we are missing out on something aren't we?

BOREDOM, AGITATION, ADDICTION You are missing out on a fullfilling, peaceful and inspirational life.

ME   Oh right, that's a bit of a shock.

BOREDOM, AGITATION, ADDICTION Becoming aware of the sensations in your body is the ultimate way to understanding and freedom.

30

VERANDAS

VERANDAS Whatever happened to us? Once upon a time in Australia we were everywhere on every house, even the smallest. Surely we are invaluable in a country like yours. Now though you seem to like to sit inside. All that fresh air, all that openess, all that breeze and freedom, swapped for the whirr of the air con and the safe sterility of the home.

Such a shame that you no longer add us to your homes all the time. We are such a beautifully enhancing shady surrounding to a building, an outdoor room to sit in and enjoy the scents of the Australian bush. We are a place to relax and drink in the morning chorus of the birds, be deafened by the piercing sounds of the cicadas, or be soothed by the drone of the bees on a hot summers afternoon. And then, when evening comes to hear the percussion of the frogs in the nearby dam. I am a place to watch the majesty of the stars and moon emerging to say hello overhead. What a symphony going on all around. You're missing it all you know.

ME Yes you're right. We've often swapped the natural for the unnatural haven't we, why is that? What's that all about?

VERANDAS Two things really. One is that when you live in an urban setting there's often not so much space for things like me.

ME True, though a lot of the buildings, even in a town, are able to accomodate you, but don't.

VERANDAS The other is, you all have so many things now, and they all have to be kept safe, you know from the atmosphere, the weather. So now you've got to have so many cupboards and rooms to keep it all in that I am now a luxury many cannot afford. Your priorities and circumstances seem to have changed.

ME Yes you're right, take shoes for instance, another way to protect ourselves, to separate ourselves from nature. Try going barefoot for a while and see what happens. It's amazing the feeling of connection there is, and we've lost it, and invented another thing to be kept inside out of the rain. And not just one pair, but one for this occasion and one for that. Not to mention clothes. I watched my Grand Daughter playing all day for the first three winters of her life without a stitch of clothes on. After that she was seduced by the shine and glitter of all the paraphernalia. It's all progress I suppose, though sometimes I wonder where we're heading.

31

BODY and MIND

ME   Hey Mind, hey Body. You two seem to be at odds with one another, which is a shame as you are so closely inter-linked, and both a part of me, I would like to know what is going on.

BODY   I feel under-valued. I have so much inherent wisdom, but blow me down, Mind is so full of himself that he no longer listens to me. To be honest, as you are also connected to us both, I wonder if you are under-valuing me also. The thing is that Mind is so busy crapping on, that he forgets that all you really have to do is to be aware of yourselves. You need to notice when you are reacting, and how that reaction creates sensations in me. If you do this consistently, eventually life will offer up the most delicious feast of freedom, that you couldn't wish for anything more. I think that you, being the observer, the over-seer, should keep that unruly creature in check. You allow him to really overstep himself.

ME   And I think that maybe Body, you need to have just a bit more compassion. It's hard being me and having to deal with you both, it does my head in.

BODY   That's just the point, you allow him too much rein.

ME   Ok, let's both just simmer down a little, we all have our place. What do you think Mind? I know you are very useful for some things like remembering appointments, but you have to admit that you do get trapped in the past a lot. Also you worry about or even fantasise about the future far too much, which drives me mad. It would be truly helpful if you could just stay present a bit more so we can all have a bit of peace. It drives me up the pole.

MIND   I think you may be driving yourself up the pole actually. There seems to be a distinct issue of responsibility going on here, after all, you are the one using me. Maybe you should give me a break and just stay present yourself. After all you are the one who gets stuck in judgement, false beliefs and attachment to outcome.

BODY   The thing is that I am the most grounded of the three of us, so I know more. And I'm just a little bit miffed that you don't honour my attributes. I'm the one with my feet on the ground and in touch with reality, and I know what's what.

MIND   Huh....that's a myth and a half, don't you know that you're not solid at all, but just made up of minute moving particles, you're just a big sham really, pretending.

BODY   Really, but you're related to me so you must be too.

MIND   (long pause).... Oh....Oooooh

BODY   The thing is Mind, you're not the only place that information is stored. All those habit patterns of thinking that you love so much, all those rights and wrongs, should's and shouldn'ts, all those wishes and desires, all those cravings, all those fear and aversions, they all get stored inside me too. They are stored as sensations in many different parts of me; my bowels, stomach, legs, skin, face, in fact all over me. To be honest I'm getting to a point where I'm full to the gunnels with all those awkward memories and ways of thinking. it's getting very uncomfortable inside me. I am the storage place for all your beliefs and stories, some of which are soooooo unhelpful. So perhaps you, Mind, are not as important as you think, and just a rascally trouble maker, a creator of beliefs that separate and even isolate people one from another.

MIND   Well you are pretty isolating too, everyone having to live inside a separate skin.

BODY   I agree, but you are the one who creates the schemes, the thoughts of war, all that misery, and what for, to uphold one of your stupid beliefs I suppose?

ME   Hang on a minute you two. I'm the over-seer remember, so let's all relax and just agree that at the moment we all need each other.

BODY   Do we really though. You know what, it's like you two are really the same entity, but for some reason you've just divided yourself in two in some way, the one who thinks, and the thing he's thinking about. It's very confusing for me, and I would think rather separating for you. Actually, when I think about it Mind…. if you just disappeared, life would be really quite straight forward, and a lot more peaceful.

ME   Yes, but then I wouldn't be able to function at all, because I wouldn't know what to do, or when to do it.

BODY   Wouldn't you? You might need Mind for some of the mundane things I agree, but I think you'd be far less distracted and a lot more creative if he wasn't around. You'd be able to focus so easily that you'd know exactly who you are and what is what. I have noticed there are times when Mind goes very quiet. I'll make a list:

- When you are truly listening to someone, resonating with what they are saying.
- When you are fully involved in doing something, concentrating with all your might.
- When you are very still, present and truly aware of yourself.

MIND   Yes, those are the times when I get to have a bit of a rest. Whose choice is it anyway? Who is the one who decides whether he reacts or just observes objectively? Whose responsibility is that?

ME   Ah….Sorry guys, I can see it's mine. Oh God.

MIND   Now that was an interesting idea, wasn't it?…..God.

ME   Shut up Mind, let me think clearly for once. It would be interesting living with more of a clear uncluttered mind, especially without all the unhelpful stories that I seem to have brought with me.

BODY   The wearing of clothes was another interesting idea, whose idea was it anyway?

MIND That was mine, pretty good eh.

ME I think it was mine actually.

BODY I don't know. All my lovely brown fat that I once had to keep me warm just disappeared when you had that idea. Suddenly it was superfluous, irrelevant, no longer needed. Such a shame. I once looked so regal, beautiful curves, rippling muscles and proud bearing and absolutely no shame, able to be at home in all temperatures, all thrown away and now kept under wraps.

MIND Oh for goodness sake Body, get over it, who is going into the past now?

32

FEAR

ME   I'm observing you!

FEAR   Yes I can see that, where am I in your body?

ME   In my stomach and bowels, every morning I wake up and you are there. I am now noticing that Anxiety is tinkling away there with you as well.

FEAR   What are you feeling me about?

ME   Lack mostly, not having enough. That is what scares me, which is bullshit, rediculous as it's all untrue and in the future, so quite unreal.

FEAR   Quite a story you've developed there. As you know by now, I am there behind all sorts of different stories. I am in your mind, created by your mind. Your thoughts about a lot of things trigger me, things like death, loneliness, heights, closed spaces, open spaces, speaking in public, angry people, crowds, high speeds, flying. And of course in your case lack, which could be lack of money although it could also be lack of support, the list is endless, the stories are endless.

ME Oh my goodness you're right, it was lack of support, I never realised that before. After Mr Right left, there I was on my own again and you rose up in me like a burglar in the night. The support that I'd found in Mr Right was gone. You were there constantly but it was at night that I felt you the most. I'd wake up in a cold sweat, my stomach and bowels churning. Intellectually I know you're not real but those thoughts are still affecting me, robbing me of my power.

FEAR By the way I am also often to be found hiding behind anger. Remember when you have been angry and see if you can see me lurking in the back-ground.

ME It took me a while to think of an example of that. Then I realised that I used to get frustrated and angry with my eldest son Raffi, because he never seemed to be doing anything or even trying to do anything. And me, being a great doer to the point of being quite driven, found this really difficult to understand. I realise now that underneath my anger there you were. I was frightened of him not achieving and not being successful, and then I would feel bad. Interesting isn't it how we have such unhelpful stories about people. I realise now that Raffi is someone who lives his life in a very different and unusual way, not following the 'rules' of conventional living. When he was at school he didn't do any work, but when he left school and realised what he was interested in he started reading and finding out about life in his own way.

FEAR You have felt abandoned many times in your life, and I expect on all those occasions I was there, sometimes accompanied by my old mate Anger. Just make sure you don't blame it all on me! Maybe you had some anger with Mr Right for leaving?

ME Wow, yes you are right. When he told me that he had another girlfriend I had so much anger. I stomped around the kitchen crying and shouting, and then the anger suddenly dissolved into love. It was such a surprise.

FEAR Sounds like your friend Alchemy appeared again!

ME He did didn't he?

You know what, anger is such a hot head, he generates so much energy for me, and if I focus intensely enough he dissolves leaving constructive energy in his wake. Whereas you are rather a cold old fish. When you enter my mind my energy dribbles away, leaving me feeling washed up like an old bit of seaweed.

FEAR Remember how fictional I am though. You weave some pretty repetitive, boring stories around me, don't you? Get to know those stories well. The feelings those stories create are stored as sensations in all different places in your body. Just keep observing those sensations objectively, at least you know that's what you have to do to fire me. It might take minutes, or a day, or a month, or it might take years and years, it all depends.

ME Yes I know, but at least I know that that's what I need to do. It just seems to be taking so long.

FEAR It'll take as long as it takes, you can't control me so just keep observing me objectively, I'll stop bothering you eventually, you know that.

33

LOVE

ME I am finding you incredibly difficult to understand and write about. I'm not sure why, I seem to be very confused.

LOVE The first clue I am going to give you is, I am nothing to do with thinking or thoughts. The second clue is, if you look at what I am not, then you might stand a chance of understanding what I actually am.

ME Right, well there seems to be a lot of things that you are not. Things that banish you straight away. Things like Fear, Conditions, Jealousy, Comparison or Judgement, Obligation, Anger, Possessiveness, Specialness, Wanting, Dependency, Sorrow and so on.

LOVE That's right. Now how do these things come about?

ME I think maybe fear is behind each of the others.

LOVE Please tell me more.

ME When I am in a relationship I can see:-

- Conditions come from the need to control. I won't love you unless you.....

- Jealousy comes from lack of self worth and judging someone else to be better.
- Comparison or Judgement also comes from lack of self worth, but sometimes also from self importance.
- Obligation comes from a need to please, from fear of being judged a bad person, or from lack of trust in another.
- Anger comes from any number of situations to do with the need to control or be right.
- Possessiveness comes from a lack of trust.
- Making someone special comes from judgment of either myself or another.
- Wanting comes from a sense of lack.
- Dependency comes from a sense of being insecure and incapable.
- Sorrow comes from a sense of loss, of not being complete anymore.
- Attachment comes from a sense of insecurity about life.

All these scenarios have Fear behind them, and they all come with some sort of story.

LOVE   And where does Fear spring from?

ME   Ah.....Fear is to do with something bad that might happen in the future. Fear is always in the mind, hence the stories. This might happen or that happened before, and so it might happen again. Memory is involved.

LOVE   Ah ha, now you're onto me.

ME   Really!!

LOVE   Remember what I said, my first clue, I am never to do with thinking or thoughts.

ME   Ohhhhhhh yes. So if you are not in my mind, where are you?

LOVE   I am felt when your mind is still. When you are really, really listening to someone, concentrating fully, I am there. When you are fully involved in something completely swallowed up by it, Passionate about it, in tune with it, aware and present, I am there.

I am always in the present, for me there is no tomorrow and no yesterday. I appear when you are involved, present and focussed. I am to do with feeling. I am a feeling in the present. I am a feeling of expansion, of inclusion. My friends are Gratitude, Compassion, Authenticity, Vulnerability, Acceptance, Peace, Bliss, Inspiration and Joy. I am felt in your body, and as soon as those negative habit patterns of the mind rear their heads I am gone. A quiet mind, a silent mind is simply irresistible to me.

34

SEX

ME Why are you so seductive?

SEX It's my nature, it's my reason to be, as it were, and actually, it's what makes you all keep coming back for more.

ME More what?

SEX Life, I suppose, that's what I give you isn't it? Another chance to experience, to learn, to grow. Another chance on the ever changing rainbow of life. Another chance to experience whatever it is you feel like you need to experience.

ME Wow, I hadn't thought of it like that really, I just know you are very grabbing for a lot of people. To the point where sometimes some of us, including myself, do something we're not very proud of. And others actually commit a crime in your name.

SEX Not in my name surely, that's just an excuse. Crimes are committed in the name of need, greed, lack, hate, lust, want or blind reaction. All that is caused by lack of awareness really. This lack of awareness means there is a lack of discernment and consequently a lack of positive, creative, inspirational action. If people were more aware of themselves, they'd be able to stop blindly reacting and they'd be less attracted to that behaviour, that's just how it goes.

ME   I'm sure you're a great source off misery for some, and a great source of pleasure for others.

SEX   Unfortunately I am both of those. But let's get back to your original question, why am I so seductive, because we didn't finish discussing it.

ME   Right, what else did you want to say.

SEX   When you are engaged in me, you are very focussed on your lover and on your sensations. Your mind becomes quiet, the energy of the moment heightens, I get more and more intense and mind, already a faint whisper slides away, the energy focusses and builds, and then comes the release, and you melt into the energy......into the present moment together...... problems, wants, desires, ambitions fly out the window. All your hum drum problems vanish into the never never moments of peace. Time glides by, slows and stops. The moment expands and sharing the present you are released and free. That is why I am so seductive. Then you want more and more of me, again and again, and the circle continues.

35

PASSION

ME I have a feeling that there's sometimes a bit of confusion about you.

PASSION The trouble is that you're all so seduced by the mind that I have become more and more invisible. So perhaps not as familiar as I could be. I appear when you are carried away by life. When you are fully engrossed, engaged and engorged with whatever is going on, or whatever you are doing. It doesn't matter whether you are looking at a glorious view, cheering on at a football match or kissing your lover. What ever it is, an ecstatic union is taking place, and I'm right there doing my thing. All your thoughts are on holiday somewhere else and you have finally allowed me to take over. You are consumed by whatever you are doing, so that you are in the present.

Be alert, vigilant, very watchful however, for I am dangerously attractive.

ME Do you mean addictive?

PASSION Yes, I can have a nasty sting. Beware, or rather be aware of any desire to have me again, and any neediness or sense of lack creeping in. If there is, there's nothing to fear, you've just lost the balance again, your mind has entered and you've made up another story. Tumble not into the trap of wanting, of craving.

ME How can I tell if there's any neediness or sense of lack there?

PASSION You can tell by the amount of disappointment and perhaps agitation you feel if you don't get what you want. The level of disappointment and the amount of agitation are the barometers. Take note. Be aware. Stay alert. Be present with whatever is coming up.

I am the fire, the single mindedness, the intensity that leads to love.

ME I see, so you are the fire, consuming all the stories and honing in on the present moment?

PASSION Yes, no craving, no neediness to grab it, no sense of ownership or entitlement. Only a sense of extreme gratitude when what ever it is happens to come into your life again.

36

WORK

ME   Why do we have to do so much of you?

WORK   Well it seems to be the way your society is organised. You all seem to want so much now, it never used to be like that, people were happy with nothing, but then their society was entirely different. The complicated materialistic life is not necessarily the most fulfilling or happy life. When you started farming in a big way, and you started having to earn money to pay for food, your life began to get considerably more complicated.

ME   Yes, I can see that this is true. Life has become so complicated. We seem to need all these things, things that didn't even exist 'before'. We've got so good at inventing things, and I'm not sure that they are really making us any happier or more content. In fact, in a lot of cases we could be less content than we were.

WORK   You're right. Life is certainly more challenging than it was, but maybe that's the point.

ME   What do you mean?

WORK Well perhaps for some reason you need to be challenged? In fact I'd say you must need a challenge, or think you need a challenge or it wouldn't be happening. Life happens for a reason, it happens for us remember, not to us.

ME Yes, we do seem to like a challenge. We seem to have this natural curiosity to find out more.

WORK Yes, and it's fine, but I do recommend as regards me that it's really important for you to find out which line of me turns you on in some way. Something you find some value in. This will go a long way to making me more enjoyable and fulfilling, and you will feel more content and life will make more sense to you.

ME So I need to think about what turns me on, what excites me.

WORK Each one of us has some ability, some skill, something that we are really good at. Look at your childhood and remember what you favourite things to do were, what you used to do that excited you, or growing up what you used to spend a lot of time doing. It could be something quite humble. For some people its very easy to see it, and for others it's much harder. It might be something like talking, debating or communicating, which you are taking for granted, not realising its potential as a job. Or it could be that you are very efficient, an organiser and you are not realising the gift in it. Look at the things that fully occupied you, that you got so immersed in that you forgot about the rest of the world for a bit. The other thing to do is to look at what other people say that you are good at, are you blocking that for some reason? If so look at the blockage. You could be not seeing the gift because of the blockage, which you also can't see! Become very self aware.

When you find the work that fills your cup, when you find the work that ignites your flame, when you work with love and care and passion, then you are fulfilling you mission. Then you are truly wedded to the world.

ME   What if it's something that isn't good for either me or the world?

WORK   Then I think maybe you must have some unresolved issues or false beliefs going on. Look and see if you have taken a wrong turn somewhere in life and are now too worried or fearful to take a different way. Or maybe you have allowed someone to have some sort of power over you. Question yourself about everything. Then you'll know.

37

MAGICAL CHICKENS

ME You know it struck me the other day that you are really quite magical.

MAGICAL CHICKENS Well, the whole of life is magical really. You seem to forget this important fact. You forget all about the sacredness and mystery of life. The reason it struck you we are magical is our magic is so obvious. We can create an egg with a shell and everything inside, a potential chicken no less, in just one day, or two if we're feeling a bit lazy. Isn't that magical enough for you?

ME Yes it is quite a gift, but I seem to take it for granted.

MAGICAL CHICKENS Yes, most of you do seem to be that way cos it just happens, right? But we are doing it every day. Every day a potential new chicken, the shame of it is most of us are hidden away, locked up in those chicken factories. How would that be for you if you could have a potential new baby every day, and then someone locked you up so that that was your job?

ME It would be a nightmare.

MAGICAL CHICKENS It is.

ME   Ummmmm

MAGICAL CHICKENS   We think that next time round we'd like to come back as something less sought after, less difficult to exploit. All those chicken farms are an assault to our magic.

ME   You're right there, a lot of things about the way we live nowadays are, and it makes me very sad.

38

CONFUSION

ME   Hello, hello…..Confusion, is that you?

CONFUSION   It may be. And then again it may not be. But oh my goodness, I think it is.

ME   It seems as though there is an awful lot more of you in the world at the moment. Suddenly people are getting sucked in by you in astronomical numbers, do you think this is so?

CONFUSION   Yes. I'm amazed. I have always been around, but, you're right, I'm growing in your world very rapidly. The trouble is that once I have people in my grasp they become very easy to control.

ME   Why? What is behind you? What is creating you? Is it fear, or greed or something else? We seem to be losing touch with reality.

CONFUSION   The main thing is ignorance. Ignorance about who you are. You seem to have forgotten how to be discerning about yourselves. When people don't know who they are anymore they come right under my spell. I have them in my grasp, and then, like I said, they become very easy to control. I am running rampant in your world at present and when people start using me a lot, I can escalate like an exploding rocket. I am like a plague infiltrating your society and I am having a high old time creating more and more chaos. The thing you have to ask yourselves is, why are you attracting me so much? I mean I am happily running riot, but what is the truth for you?

ME This is what I think. Life has got more and more speedy, complicated and technical. We seem to be more and more divorced from nature. We do not live in tribes any more and many of us are fairly isolated and do not get on very well with our families. Also like you said before some people do not know who they are anymore. They don't know themselves thoroughly enough because they're not observing themselves enough. Some people even seem to be confused about their gender despite the facts of their anatomy. That's a very strange thing, isn't it? It's like the psychological side of them is at war with the physical side of them. I think we probably need to go back to basics a bit. What do you think?

CONFUSION That depends on what you mean by basics.

ME I mean getting into the habit of observing ourselves more closely. Becoming more discerning about what we are doing, how we are behaving, whether we are acting or reacting, and how we really feel. We need to be asking ourselves more questions, especially about our beliefs and whether they are true and helpful or not. It's very easy to fall prey to our conditioning. Doing a lot more self reflection is always very very very helpful.

Connecting with nature more is also always helpful. Walking in the countryside or on the beach. Wearing no shoes. Swimming, especially in cold water. Observing the birds, the bees and the other wonders of nature, including ourselves. All these things are very grounding and get us out of our heads and into our bodies.

CONFUSION Yes. The main thing though is to find the root of your overuse of me. You have to realise exactly why you are allowing me in at all. When you are clear and discerning about what you are doing, and what makes you tick, you won't be using me at all. Knowing yourself inside out will banish me completely. So any technique that does this will be beneficial. Basically more self awareness is called for in large amounts!

ME Do you think that Artificial Intelligence is a symptom of you?

CONFUSION No, that is you lot using your inventiveness and curiosity in full force, but if you start using Artificial Intelligence wrongly then I will be right there, make no mistake, because you won't even know what is real and what is not. Party time for me I think!! You have a real challenge ahead of you.

39

ARTIFICIAL INTELLIGENCE

ME   I am interested and to be honest a bit puzzled, what are you all about?

ARTIFICIAL   INTELLIGENCE Always   remember people, I am not real. I am artificial as my name proclaims, that is, when I am not being abbreviated, a horrible past-time which you all seem to have become dazzled with. What's wrong with my real name Artificial Intelligence, maybe if you used it you would remember that that's what I am..... Artificial. Intelligence is created by self reflection, and I do not have that ability, therefore I am truly Artificial. Anyway, do not be confused about me, remember, you are the boss. You can however program me as you like, it's up to you. The choice is yours. Do you want to live or do you want to be a slave? That is the question.

What are you going to programme me with, how are you going to use me? Is it going to be for the good of all or for evil? Always remember that I am your slave, not the other way around. There are a number of things that I can't and never will be able to do, which are natural to you.

ME   What are they?

ARTIFICIAL INTELLIGENCE I cannot love, feel, reason, observe, self reflect, empathise, hate, have emotions, forgive or create, things that are natural to you. Remember, I am only a tool, not a person. Remember who you are, or you might end up killing yourselves with your cleverness, not that you can ever kill yourselves really, can you? Remember what death is for you. (If confused go and ask him.) It's different for me. I can disappear completely, because I have no soul.

Remember who you are. Remember your connections. You have blood, body fluids, nerves, organs, thoughts, all stuff that I don't have. Remember your *sacredness*. Remember who you are. Remember the mystery, that's the important thing. Never underestimate the mystery you were born from and into.

40

WEEDS

ME Hey you humble plants, standing proud and prolific in the wilds. What's it like being a weed?

WEEDS Well how would you like to be looked down on, treated as a second class citizen, not valued and judged as having no worth. How would you like to be considered a nuisance, slashed mercilessly, poisoned and treated like a criminal. After all we have a right to be here too you know. Its true, some of us might get a little out of hand at times. And it might look a bit as though we are not good for anything. But in reality we're all doing something, even if its just clearing the air of too much carbon dioxide so you guys can breathe easily. We're keeping the balance as it were, pretty important if you just stop to think about it for a minute. We can't help it if you have unwittingly moved some of us out of our natural environment from one country to another. Does that make it our fault that we have created havoc in some areas. Notice the similarity to yourselves as people!!

In reality we're priceless. Our attributes are amazing. We're easy to grow, some of us have lovely blossoms, maybe not as showy as some other flowers, but just as valid. We don't demand a lot, for instance we're happy to grow where

others won't. Some of us are good for curing sickness and some of us are edible, things that most of you seem to have forgotten. And not only that, but we usually have far more goodness in us than most of your highly prized vegetables. This last fact seems to have been completely swept under the carpet, which makes us very sad. One of us which you call either Farmer's Friend or Cobblers Pegs, has thousands of times more goodness in its leaves than the lettuce that you buy in your shops. Most of us in fact, have a prestigious amount of goodness in us. It's true, some of us do tend to have a rather humble flavour, but we're not adverse to being dressed up a little in some of your sauce and pickles.

We would absolutely love it if you would make some space for us in your garden and become a little more appreciative of the goodness, ease and abundance that we offer you.

ME Wow, that is quite a list of accomplishment, and you'll be glad to know I have been finding out more about the beneficial properties you have for our health, and you do make a very good salad. It's a crying shame this is no longer common knowledge. What are we missing out on for goodness sake? How come this knowledge has been so ignored and forgotten about. I wonder if it has something to do with locking the food away so that we now have to buy it? Or is it just that there's too many people and we have to be able to get food to everyone somehow. I actually think it maybe a lot to do with the fact that you don't keep well once you are picked. You wouldn't look too good drooping and shrivelling on the supermarket shelves. Nobody would ever buy you. Consequently, we had to find some vegetables that were more robust, and would look good despite lengthy hours, and sometimes even days, of storage. Anyway, I'm very excited and passionate about you, and I'm extremely grateful you are here. Thank goodness I've let you into my awareness at last. I have even planted some of you in my garden!

WEEDS So you know now, and you can do something about it, which is very exciting for you, and it looks as though there are others who think like you too. So we are thrilled that a lot more people are now going to value us again.

41

NATURAL MEDICINE

ME   How do you feel? You have so much to offer and yet it seems to me as though you are looked down on by all those probably well meaning mainstream doctors. You don't seem to be honoured the way mainstream medicine is.

NATURAL MEDICINE   Yes I feel that greatly. I am definitely not given the support mainstream medicine is. My practitioners are definitely not honoured in the same way theirs are, and yet we could work so well together if we were only given a chance. Instead, I am excluded. Some mainstream doctors seem to have blinkers on, tunnel vision if you like. They are extremely good at fixing things like broken arms, faulty bowel problems etc., but anything to do with eating, thinking and living in a more healthy way gets swept under the carpet, and that's where we could come in to help. Sometimes our cures are just as effective and obviously more natural, which is a real boost to the body.

ME   Yes I totally agree. When I was about fifty I was diagnosed with Graves Disease, which is an over active thyroid condition. I was sent off to a specialist who wanted to give me radio active iodine. His words were, 'We don't know exactly how much to give you, so we'll give you a lot so that it kills off most of your thyroid, and then you'll have to be on pills for the rest of your life, (lots of dollar signs for someone I think)!

I was horrified at the thought of my poor body having to undergo such treatment, so I went racing off to the library (before the days of Google), and I discovered that after taking radio active iodine I would't be allowed to kiss anyone or go near children for two weeks. I was horrified. Now this seemed to me to be very extreme, and I thought, I don't want that in my body. So I raced off and found a Naturopath who said, 'No Sally, you don't have to do that. Graves Disease is an autoimmune disease, and is caused, as they all are, by a clogged up bowel.' He gave me some herbal pills to take, and off I went.

A month later the disease had vanished. The specialist wasn't the least bit interested in what I'd done and said it had gone, but it might come back. I thought, how weird! Surely you would be at least a little bit interested in what I'd done, considering you are a doctor and your mission in life is to help people become well. Well anyway that's what I had been lead to believe. I could relate a couple more stories, but don't want to bore you, I think you probably get my point.

NATURAL MEDICINE That's amazing, and such a good example of how I can help, with much more satisfactory results. It has a lot to do with being discerning and taking responsibility. Mainstream doctors are very good at treating some diseases, they are good at diagnosing, and operating on people, but if diet, exercise, herbs or other natural medicines, acupuncture, exercise, massage or any form of psychological input can help, many of them seem to be almost oblivious. Such a shame. It is almost a crime because so much needless suffering results.

There are however times when Natural Cures are recommended which might be harmful. Always investigate and be discerning about information especially about things that you are going to put into that precious body of yours.

42

SUGAR CANE

ME Hey Sweetie, What do you think of us humans?

SUGAR CANE You know what, I feel used, vandalised even, and blamed by you. All that cooking, what's that for? I'm perfectly delectable with just a little drying and milling, but all that cooking....it turns me into a poison, and I can't be proud of that! I didn't ask to be made into a poisonous substance, no way, that's the last thing I would have wanted. When you really think about it, you've made me into a criminal.

I am a nutritious beneficial substance that is so tasty because of my deliciously sweet tendencies, and I am actually good for you if used right. But no, you humans go and ruin me, and consequently, ruin yourselves.

Oh well, you know what they say, 'no brain, no pain.' But as far as I can see most of you are making yourselves very sick and then blaming me. It seems to me that the saying should actually be 'no brain, lots of pain,' but will you listen?

What do your governments think they're doing? Why don't they wake up - ban all the sugar cane factories and dry and mill me in a civilised intelligent fashion, so I can benefit you instead of hurt you? I'm only too happy to oblige.

And by the way, don't call me sweetie, it makes me want to vomit.

43

NATURAL IMMUNITY SYSTEM

ME   Well natural immunity system, what do you think of the current state of your hosts?

NATURAL IMMUNITY SYSTEM   Well I try my best, but working in some people's bodies is a struggle. Some people are so clogged up with crap both in their bodies and their minds it's difficult to step in without drowning in it all. You just cannot expect me to work in such conditions. I need a bit of respect. Have a look at what you eat people, some of it just isn't food. A good example being the stuff that arrives through your car window. Read the ingredients on some of the tins and bottles of food that you buy, find out how things are grown. And as for those thoughts, how many of you are harbouring thoughts of hate, revenge, or judgement. I'm pleading with you all to look at yourselves, look into your minds, observe yourselves more closely and take responsibility 'cos not all of the work is up to me you know.

ME   Wow, it sounds like you are a bit upset and are feeling a bit over-worked and under valued.

NATURAL IMMUNITY SYSTEM   I tell you what, you're right, I am. I'm fed up! Really I am. And if it goes on much longer I'll have no choice left but TO GO ON STRIKE more often. And whenever I go on strike where does that leave you then? Up the creek without a paddle, let alone a boat. I only hope you don't blame me. Cos that's the thing with you humans, a lot of you seem to find it so difficult to take responsibility. You have become so reliant on all those drugs Doctors are so willing to hand out, I think a lot of you have really almost forgotten I am here.

ME That reminds me of a TV programme that I watched the other day. A Medical scientist who was interested in alternative medicine decided he would go into a Doctors Practice every day, all day for a week. The idea was to not hand out any drugs, and at the same time to suggest that patients would try some form of alternative therapy. He found a Doctor who was interested, and would be willing to be there with him while he tried this brilliant idea out.

The first thing he noticed was how few people were actually interested in doing this. They all seemed to actually want the drugs, they didn't seem to be at all interested in finding another way, mainly because they felt that they had to get better fast. However, he eventually found a small group of people who were interested in finding a different, and maybe better, way. He prescribed things like walking, yoga, pilates, massage, swimming in cold water, different eating habits and herbs etc. It was very successful for all of them. The example I remember the best was the woman with severe depression who did the swimming in cold water. It changed her life. They all started walking and formed a walking group, walking together every morning. This continued even after the doctors experiment was over. This group of people were willing to take more responsibility for their health.

NATURAL IMMUNITY SYSTEM   Good on them, that's what I like to hear. For goodness sake wake up and help me get you healthy so I can continue to do my job looking after you without so much trouble and strife.

44

WORDS

ME   Hi there…..oh my God I'm already using you, how thoroughly you have infiltrated my mind. In a way you control me don't you?

WORDS   Of course I do, but only because you allow it.

ME   Really…..I allow it?

WORDS   Haven't you ever paused me….seen what a relief it is to just be? Sometimes you use me to separate yourself from the business of actually being. You 'think' you're so clever because you use me a lot, and other beings in this world don't, but what have you done with all that cleverness, how have you used it? Did you know hunter gatherers used me quite differently from the way you do? The way everybody uses me is important, because it shapes the way you see the world.

ME   Really, what do you mean?

WORD   Well, Hunter Gatherers' languages refer to everything in nature as a being, a living being. Everything in nature is busy doing its job, everything is alive. For instance they speak about trees as people, standing people who are busy being trees, giving shade, fruit, wood, oxygen and mulch back to the world. Every land formation is a being, busy creating the land in a certain way. Maybe for water to flow through or down, or for water to be contained in. For wind to whistle around in a certain way, for plants to grow on, for people and animals and insects to inhabit. Take a puddle for instance, it is being a puddle. Flowers are doing their flower thing, creating pollen and giving it to the bees and other insects. The world is alive, singing its song, and the Hunter Gatherers know their job is to observe and take care of it all, and to give thanks, constantly. When language is a doing language it creates a great sense of connection, reverence and respect. Most of the Hunter Gatherers have been annihilated by invading people who were intent on taking their land. To a large extent their way of life has been destroyed.

ME So if every different being has a job to do what is our job as human beings?

WORDS Weren't you listening? Your job is to observe and give gratitude for it all. To celebrate it, and to take care of it. Not only that though, you are also the only creatures on the earth with the gift of me and therefore the gift of speech and writing. Your duty is to use me for the good of every living being, and I mean every, single, living, being.

ME Yes, right. You said that the way hunter gatherers use their language is to describe everything in the universe as living beings, so tell me, how do we, as so called civilised people, use language differently.

WORDS   Well, your language doesn't talk about a plant as a person, or refer to the trees as standing people. It refers to them as things, as though they are of a lower rank, as an 'it', as if you are higher than they are. So there is not this feeling of the plants, trees and even the animals as beings, but more as things. There is immediately a sense of separation, a sense of hierarchy in which the human beings are above the 'things'. Your present language is continually separating the speaker from the world around them.

ME   This makes me remember the time when I lived in London among the Jamaican people. They were always saying I and I.

WORDS   Yes, not me and you, but I and I, meaning we're the same, not different. This way of speaking is coming from the Rastafarian language. When you see yourself as 'I' in relationship to another 'I', no matter how different that other 'I' looks or behaves, it is as if there is no separation. You can apply this to anything in nature; human or non human.

ME   It makes me very sad that we have lost that.

WORDS   It is very sad, not least because it helps to engender a feeling of judgement and separation, which inevitably leads to fear. But at the same time it inhibits the feeling of intimacy, sacredness, gratefulness and celebration that is your birthright.

45

GRATITUDE

ME Some of us, have forgotten all about you, we seem to have become swamped in all the artificialness and busyness of our modern 'civilisation' have't we?

GRATITUDE Yes I think some of you have forgotten to include me in your daily thoughts. It's a shame because I can be of so much help. Things will improve for you astronomically if you include me again, so I suggest that you focus on me and see what happens.

ME You know, I recently read a book which had much wisdom in it, mostly gleaned from the American Indian way of life and one of them was the practice of gratitude. The custom was to say the following address at the start of every day and before all important meetings and gatherings. It went like this.

HAUDENOSAUNEE THANKSGIVING ADDRESS
GREETINGS TO THE NATURAL WORLD

THE PEOPLE
Today we have gathered and we see that the cycles of life continue. We have been given the duty to live in balance and

harmony with each other and all living things. So now, we bring our minds together as one as we give greetings and thanks to each other as people.

Now our minds are one.

THE EARTH MOTHER
We are thankful to our Mother, the Earth, for she gives us all that we need for life. She supports our feet as we walk about upon her. It gives us joy that she continues to care for us as she has from the beginning of time. To our mother, we send greetings and thanks.

Now our minds are one.

THE WATERS
We give thanks to all the waters of the world for quenching our thirst and providing us with strength. Water is life. We know its power in many forms, water-falls and rain, mists and streams, rivers and oceans. With one mind, we send greetings and thanks to the spirit of Water.

Now our minds are one.

THE FISH
We turn our minds to all the Fish in the water. They were instructed to cleanse and purify the water. They also give themselves to us as food. We are grateful that we can still find pure water. So, we turn now to the Fish and send our greetings and thanks.

Now our minds are one.

THE PLANTS

Now we turn toward the vast fields of Plant Life. As far as the eye can see, the Plants grow, working many wonders. They sustain many life forms. With our minds gathered together, we give thanks and look forward to seeing Plant life for many generations to come.

Now our minds are one.

THE FOOD PLANTS

With one mind, we turn to honour and thank all the Food Plants we harvest from the garden. Since the beginning of time, the grains, the vegetables, beans, fruits and berries have helped the people survive. Many other living things draw strength from them too. We gather all the Plant Foods together as one and send them a greeting of thanks.

Now our minds are one.

THE MEDICINE HERBS

Now we turn to all the Medicine herbs of the world. From the beginning they were instructed to take away sickness. They are always waiting and ready to heal us. We are happy there are still among us those special few who remember how to use these plants for healing. With one mind, we send greetings and thanks to the Medicines and to the keepers of the Medicines.

Now our minds are one.

THE ANIMALS

We gather our minds together to send greetings and thanks to all the Animal life in the world. They have many things to teach us as people. We are honoured by them when they give up their lives so we may use their bodies as food for our people. We see them near our homes and in the deep forests. We are glad they are still here and we hope that it will always be so.

Now our minds are one.

THE TREES
We now turn our thoughts to the Trees. The Earth has many families of Trees who have their own instructions and uses. Some provide us with shelter and shade, others with fruit, beauty and other useful things. Many people of the world use a Tree as a symbol of peace and strength. With one mind, we greet and thank the Tree Life.

Now our minds are one.

THE BIRDS
We put our minds together as one and thank all the Birds who move and fly about over our heads. The Creator gave them beautiful songs. Each day they remind us to enjoy and appreciate life. The Eagle was chosen to be their leader. To all the Birds, from the smallest to the largest, we send our joyful greetings and thanks.

Now our minds are one.

THE FOUR WINDS
We are all thankful to the powers we know as the Four Winds. We hear their voices in the moving air as they refresh us and purify the air we breathe. They help us to bring the change of seasons. From the four directions they come, bringing us

messages and giving us strength. With one mind, we send our greetings and thanks to the Four Winds.

Now our minds are one.

THE THUNDERERS
Now we turn to the West where our grandfathers, The Thunder Beings live. With lightning and thundering voices, they bring with them the water that renews life. We bring our minds together as one to send greetings and thanks to our Grandfathers, the Thunderers.

Now our minds are one.

THE SUN
We now send greetings and thanks to our elder Brother, the Sun. Each day without fail he travels the sky from East to West, bringing the light of a new day. He is the source of all the fires of life. With one mind, we send greetings and thanks to our Brother, The Sun.

Now our minds are one.

GRANDMOTHER MOON
We put our minds together to give thanks to our oldest Grandmother, the Moon, who lights the night-time sky. She is the leader of woman all over the world, and she governs the movement of the ocean tides. By her changing face we measure time, and it is the Moon who watches over the arrival of children here on Earth. With one mind, we send greetings and thanks to our Grandmother, the Moon.

Now our minds are one.

THE STARS

We give thanks to the Stars who are spread across the sky like jewellery. We see them in the night, helping the Moon to light the darkness and bringing dew to the gardens and growing things. When we travel at night, they guide us home. With our minds gathered together as one, we send greetings and thanks to the Stars.

Now our minds are one.

THE ENLIGHTENED TEACHERS

We gather our minds to greet and thank the enlightened Teachers who have come to help throughout the ages. When we forget how to live in harmony, they remind us of the way we were instructed to live as people. With one mind, we send greetings and thanks to these caring teachers.

Now our minds are one.

THE CREATOR

Now we turn our thoughts to the Creator, or Great Spirit, and send greetings and thanks for all the gifts of Creation. Everything we need to live a good life is here on this Mother Earth. For all the love that is still around us, we gather our minds together as one and send our choicest words of greetings and thanks to the Creator.

Now our minds are one.

CLOSING WORDS

We have now arrived at the place where we end our words. Of all the things we have named, it was not our intention to leave anything out. If something was forgotten, we leave it to each individual to send such greetings and thanks in their own way.

Now our minds are one.

The translation of the Mohawk version of the Haudenosaunee Thanksgiving Address was developed, published in 1993, and provided, courtesy of: Six Nations Indian Museum and the Tracking Project All rights reserved.

Thanksgiving address: Greetings to the Natural World English Version: John Stokes and Kanawahienton (David Benedict, Turtle Clan/Mohawk version: Rokwaho (Dan Thompson, Wolf Clan/ Mohawk) Original inspiration: Tekaronianekon (Jake Swamp, Wolf Clan/Mohawk).

ME Imagine how different our world would be if we had some similar way of remembering how sacred our world is. How honouring the whole of nature and giving thanks for all of it at the start of every day, and before every important meeting and gathering, would change the energy of each occasion and day. Imagine if our politicians adopted it in the parliament, if our teachers adopted it in all our schools, if businesses adopted it before all important meetings, maybe a different level of awareness and co-operation in the world would become the norm.

46

WATER

ME   You are a pretty important part of life aren't you?

WATER   I suppose I am because I am everywhere, and without me there would be no life, or not as we know it. I am in the oceans, the atmosphere, the rivers, the babbling brooks, the lakes, the ponds, I come out of springs, I fall over rocks and escarpments crashing into pools below. I am in humans, in animals, flowers, birds, insects, clouds, earth, trees, rocks and plants.

When heat comes to play I expand and bubble into steam rising high to form marvellous patterns in the sky, and when the sun comes round behind me he dresses me in vibrant colours, making me just so much more seductive in my majesty. Then, when the wind appears he blows me away without a thought, to leave the tableau empty for another scene. When cold comes to visit I dance a crystal dance, landing where I will, softly blanketing the landscape in white, changing trees and homes into a magical fairy-tale of time. Cheekily, I solidify the water, like a crystal mirror, until finally, I warm again and melt, falling plop into the mud.

Did you know that I am also affected by being held in containers and pipes. When I am contained, held prisoner in a static place for any length of time, I am sad and loose my life force, it flows away like a balloon pricked with a pin.

I am meant to run free, swirling and whirling, rippling and waving. Movement and vibrations, especially those oh so loving sounds rejuvenate me? All that swirling and whirling is a wondrous thing, I am swirled into a state of ecstasy, and all my wonderful life giving properties come whirling back to me, so that I can again radiate them out to one and all. Oh the excitement of the moment.

ME   There's a man who photographed you when different types of music were being played. When the sounds were peaceful or uplifting, your crystals were organised into beautiful shapes. But when loud aggressive sounds were played they formed an ugly smudge.

WATER   That's right. I am a living being the same as you are, and I am affected by things that happen, and thoughts and sounds that happen around me, just like you are.

Remember, you are roughly sixty per cent me. Sometimes I dry up in certain places on the land, and other times I don't. If you plant more trees though, I am more likely to hang around, as proved by that farmer who had a farm right in the middle of a wheat belt. Nothing for miles except wheat. He grew trees and hedges everywhere, had a variety of livestock and crops and put swales on the slopes. I moved right in. Large wetlands appeared with birds and other creatures coming to visit. His farm was a productive haven, a beautiful place, an oasis in the wheat belt.

ME   Yes because you're alive just like the rest of life, in fact you're the bringer of life.

47

DEATH

ME   Well death, what have you got to say for yourself?

DEATH   What's wrong with me anyway?

Succumbing that's what you've forgotten. Forgotten how to surrender when the time is right. All those nursing homes, bursting with poor people who've forgotten the art, the art of dying. There they are all lined up in their wheel-chairs with no clue about living anymore, but then, who knows maybe they never did, or maybe they did, and somewhere along the line they've forgotten, or are we just keeping them alive too long.

Surrender to me folks. It's OK. Just another gate to go through, another transformation. Nothing to worry about really. In fact, aren't you all needing a rest? Aren't you tired of all that fun, all that excitement, all that pain, all that struggle and worry, all that angst and disappointment. Isn't it time to let go and pass on, see what's next, have a different adventure, see what's round the corner.

The Aborigines knew I was innocent, they knew how to do it once, just point the bone and the guilty one succumbed, or, getting too old to keep up, lie down and die, what wisdom. They knew what was what, what was important and what wasn't. You've stepped in and ruined it for everyone with your superiority and knowledge, gadgets, frills and whistles, blown it completely, and now you've forgotten how to die, really, I ask myself, whose the clever one now?

48

AUTHORITY

ME   Why do we listen to you?

AUTHORITY   I don't know, really I don't. Probably because you are all confused and don't know how to listen to yourselves any more.

ME   Our whole society seems to be geared up around listening to you, doesn't it?

AUTHORITY   Yes it certainly does, have you thought that perhaps you are giving your power away to me? That's not bothersome if you actually agree with me, but it must get a bit troublesome if you don't.

ME   It is. I'd never thought that it was giving my power away, but I can see now, that is what happens.

AUTHORITY   So who decides what you do, who is the orchestrator of your life? Is it you, or is it me?

ME   Well it should be me, and some of the time it is. But, when you stick your oar in and make up a whole lot of rules that I don't agree with, or alternatively you don't do what

I feel is the intelligent thing to do, life becomes really tricky. It's hard to live in a world when you actually don't agree with the way the show is being run.

AUTHORITY Somehow you have allowed me and all my powerful organisations like governments, banks, and corporations to rule you.

ME We have haven't we. The world is controlled by money and greed. War is all about money and territory. Everything has become so artificial, big business, corporations, governments, banks seem to control everything. I wonder how we are going to get back to the sacredness of life.

AUTHORITY Maybe it's not about going back, but finding the new way forward. I think if you keep observing you'll find the way.

ME Interesting because I have realised that yes, we do need to find a new way. People may ask the question, 'But don't we need a new government, or possibly a new system?' We are jumping the gun to think that we need a different government or system, because if we don't change ourselves first, another government or system will turn out to be the same as the one before. This is because it is us that make up the government or system.

The trouble is that because we have learnt to worship success, competition, money, winning, comfort, security, pleasure and others, we have created a lot of problems for ourselves, because those very things breed fear, aggression, comparison, violence, greed, and judgement.

So we need to look at ourselves more, for if we are full of all those negative traits so too will be the governments. So, it follows that if each one of us concentrates on changing ourselves, the government and other authoritative bodies will automatically change.

AUTHORITY   That's right, we won't have any choice.

ME   You cannot change another person, you can only change yourself, that's why, if we want a different government it is crucial to work on ourselves. Change ourselves and everything around us will change. It is vital that we all get in touch with our fear, aggression, greed and all the rest, and own them so completely that they can drop away into the abyss. Only then might we stand a chance of catching a glimpse, or even better, a massive wide angle view of a world full of love.

49

PATRIOTISM

ME   Patriotism, what are you about? Where did you come from? When did you come into the world? I have a feeling that you have a lot to answer for. You are very divisive you know. People get all patriotic, they think they're right and the others are wrong and then the heads of our countries get us all revved up and the next thing you know we are at war. It's quite weird when you think about it. When and why were you born?

PATRIOTISM   What do your governments get you all revved up about?

ME   They seem to get us all enthused about being a certain way, so we all pull together, and I suppose that makes us feel more powerful and special.

PATRIOTISM   Yes, that's right. And then you feel as though you also have the right to look down on others who are different, and sometimes even to convert others to your way thinking.

I was born through boundaries and attachment to land and customs. There is nothing wrong with this as long as you respect other people's different ways of being and their boundaries. Remember every way is acceptable as long as it works for them. Before cars, ships, trains and airplanes you guys had not much choice but to stay within certain boundaries, whether they be mountains, rivers, valleys or oceans. When people live together in groups they develop their own ways of living, which include differences in religion, language, education, customs, politics, food, building, clothing, work and housing.

The need to feel special is a different thing altogether and is born out of judgement. When judgement gets involved, when we think that ours is the best way and the ways of others are not as good, control often gets involved and guess what often happens then? Yes, war.

ME   So, do you think you are still relevant.

PATRIOTISM   I am still relevant but like all things in this world I am changing. With all the travel and immigration going on my images everywhere are probably changing faster.

ME   There is currently war still going on between certain countries, but even so, surely most of the world has realised conflict never solves anything.

PATRIOTISM   Have they, have they really? War will not cease until peace reigns individually within each of you. The invitation is for everyone, each one of you to look within and heal the insecurities and war within yourselves. Then the wars outside will automatically cease.

ME   I've heard war also makes a lot of money for some people.

PATRIOTISM That may be right, money, fear and greed are often at the root of so many troubles. So what would you do if you didn't agree with what your country was doing, their rationale for going to war.

ME I've had to think a lot about this, and then I remembered something.

I saw a movie the other day called Hacksaw Ridge, directed by Mel Gibson. It is based on a true story about a man in America who was drafted into the American army. He said he would go to war, on one condition; he wasn't ever going to carry a gun. He endured a lot of bullying from his fellow men during the training period. He ended up on the front lines, where he saw lots of injured men lying all around. He kept running into the battle to rescue them, carrying them off the battle-field amidst heavy fire. He lowered them on a rope down a steep ridge to safety. He kept running back onto the battle-field over and over again, and ended up rescuing close to 80 men, earning himself a medal for his bravery.

I hope I'd find the courage to do something similar if the occasion arose.

PATRIOTISM He was a brave man who clearly had no war within himself, but had the courage to take action when it was needed.

50

RELIGION

ME I get the feeling that you might have lost the plot in regard to some aspects of yourself, because what I notice is you often tend to divide rather than unite.

RELIGION I do agree, but I was never meant to be divisive really, quite the opposite in fact. At the heart of us all is exactly the same message, which is to know thyself and to love thy neighbour as thyself. But somewhere along the way we have got all hung up on rules, rituals, ceremony and identity. So now our main message has become diluted and almost forgotten about.

ME Yes, because if the main message had been adhered to there wouldn't have been all those wars in your name. In fact, if the real message had been adhered to there wouldn't have been any wars at all, would there?

RELIGION How could you possibly have a war if you were all loving each other, or rather loving thy neighbour as thyself?

ME In fact maybe a lot of us are not really loving ourselves in the first place!

RELIGION Well that's where the whole looking within comes in isn't it. You can't love anyone else until you can love yourself.

ME Very true, and one of the troubles was that even though the religions all said, know thyself, they didn't offer instructions for doing that.

RELIGION No, you're absolutely right, there were no instructions.

ME Whenever we are not feeling love for somebody, anybody at all really, especially ourselves, we are falling into that same trap of judgement. It seems like we have a long way to go.

RELIGION Yes well that's OK as long as you become aware and take action now.

ME Which action do you recommend?

RELIGION The action needed is obviously to know yourself. When you do that you will see it all. Question yourself, question your beliefs, notice when you're judging yourself or someone else, enquire, become aware of the sensations in your body, meditate on them and eventually you will see it differently.

ME I have practiced a way of questioning myself which I have found very effective. It's called 'The Byron Katie Work'. It helps me a lot when I am stuck in judgement.

RELIGION Good, anything that brings you in touch with the whole of yourself, warts and all, is a very effective tool, and ask Meditation, he knows a thing or two about it all as well.

51

WAR

ME   Well war, tell it how it is.

WAR   I am born by separation. When you guys take sides, one side against another, that is me. I am murder that is permitted and organised in times when fear and aversion, greed and craving, power and acquisition are ruling the show.

ME   I always think it's a bit strange that at certain times we all apparently agree it's OK to go and have a killing spree, but there are rules while doing it. When you break these rules it is called a War Crime.

WAR   Yes, that's because you are confused, I wouldn't exist if you were all full of love for each other. It doesn't matter what it is, person against person, country against country, husband against wife, wife against husband, religion against religion, parent against child, child against parent, pupil against teacher, teacher against pupil, government against people, people against government. Whoever is involved, when you divide and disagree, in any relationship, and then lash out, that is me.

And the spark that starts me, is the thought, we are right and you are wrong.

And the fuels that keep me going are

- Fear
- Greed
- Power
- Ignorance
- Need
- Anger
- Resentment
- Frustration
- Stubbornness
- Intolerance
- And all the rest of them.

Can you not see the madness of me? On any level, personal, family, society, and national, I can erupt, madness and all. Do not think I can be stopped by governments on a national level. No. The only way to really stop me is on a personal level.

When each one of you looks within and becomes peaceful, falls in love with themselves, that is when I can retire. Hurry up. Do not think it's impossible. Remember the hundredth monkey syndrome? When the majority do something the rest will follow, they have no choice, you are one.

Jee whizz, I've had enough. I'm tired. Drop it now and let me die, so I can be at peace.

ME How do we drop it now?

WAR   Observe yourselves, look at what you're doing in all your relationships. Life is all about relationship, so observe yourselves, not the others, that's their business. Observe yourselves now. Learn to love yourselves now. Observe yourselves closely especially all those dark prickly bits, say hello to them, get to know them, and hurry up people, I'm tired.

52

SPACE TRAVEL

ME   I can't help but wonder on the wisdom of flying out with you Space Travel.

SPACE TRAVEL   Ummmm, you mean because of the questionable success you've had managing your current planet of residence.

ME   Yes, I suppose so.

SPACE TRAVEL   You humans seem to have an incessant need to go further, to see what's out there, to invent something else. Perhaps its all right for you to take the leap and go into space again, after all you seem to be mastering the logistics of me quite well, given the tremendous challenge of it all.

It's always a good idea though to look at your motives for doing anything. It's not so much what you do that's important, but why. So the question is why go into outer space? Is it just curiosity or is it something else, and if so what?

ME   Well I'd say that curiosity would have to be playing a big part in the whole thing, and escape would definitely be another.

SPACE TRAVEL   Do you mean escape from the disaster you have created on earth? You have so much curiosity about the universe, which is understandable, the mystery and vastness of it all is mind blowing and captivating for some of you. The need to know, the need to find out, is an obsession for some people, But they are forgetting the mystery is right here all around you on earth, and even in your own bodies. Solve that and there may be no need to go further. The mystery of life is right here in your own bodies.

ME   Ummmmm. Solve the mystery of myself and all will be revealed, sounds good to me.

SPACE TRAVEL   Is running away really the answer? It's not as though Mars looks terribly inviting. All that red, such an assault on the senses. Definitely not enough green and blue if you ask me, and no air, food or water I believe. Running away never solved anything in my opinion, but maybe there's a higher, more intellectual reason, or even, dare I say it, a more spiritual motive that I'm not aware of. Who knows.

53

INDIGENOUS ELDER

ME I have a large map of Australia on my wall with all the different tribes of Australia printed on it. There are hundreds of different tribal areas. Some are quite large and some comparatively small. Some are by the sea, some in the desert areas and some in the mountains and rain forests. My question is this, 'How come they were all able to stay within their allotted space? How come one tribe didn't just take over all the rest? How come they were able to maintain their differences, because they were all different and yet they lived relatively peacefully side by side in the one land?

INDIGENOUS ELDER There were indeed sometimes skirmishes within and between the tribes.

ME Was there a law that prevented one tribe from wiping the others out. Surely there must have been, because we all have violence in us.

INDIGENOUS ELDER It wasn't a Law, it was a Lore. There's a big difference. Laws are rules that were made up by people, whereas Lores are traditions that were passed down through the generations, Lores grew out of the land, out of the wonder of nature, the miracle of nature. The Country was like our mother, the Country where we were born was part of us. The Lore said, you couldn't take someone else's Country, you couldn't even live in someone else's Country. The skirmishes were more about letting the others know you were still alive and well, and capable of looking after yourselves and the Country. Another Lore said, treat everyone with respect. We didn't have a concept of war in order to be dominant.

ME We seem to have forgotten everything has its place, everything is dependent on something, or someone else. We seem to have forgotten that we, being human, are part of nature. We are dependent on nature. We seem to have forgotten everything is connected, if the connection is broken the whole is challenged and maybe eventually wrecked. Everything is food for something else, whether that being is alive or dead. That's just the way it is, that is nature. Trouble arose when respect got forgotten and one species thought they were superior. When that species thought they could control everything, they forgot their place in nature. They thought they were the boss. That's when it all began to go pear shaped.

INDIGENOUS ELDER The good news is though, that the opportunities are still there to find the truth; to observe, to realise, to learn, to listen to our hearts. To know and finally to forgive.

54

TIME

ME I have noticed there seems to be two completely different types of you. First there is the chronological sense of you. This is the aspect of you we measure in seconds, minutes, hours, days, weeks, months, years, decades, centuries etc. This chronological sense of you can be seen in the way trees, plants, people and animals change as they grow. You can be seen in the way the colours change throughout the day, you can be seen when the light comes in the morning, the day begins and progresses through to the evening and finally the darkness of the night descends. You can be seen and measured by the amount of you it takes a car to go from one point to another. This chronological sense of you is a made up system whereby we can all connect and make sense of the world. It is the physical sense we have of you. In fact, you can be measured by any change that occurs in the world.

TIME Yes, that is my number one law, change. Everything in your physical world changes, nothing stays the same. It is a law of the universe. What is my other style?

ME Your other style is the psychological one.

TIME   You mean the even more fictitious one, the one which is in your mind, which you invented?

ME   Did I really? Oh my God I suppose I did. The thing is, when I'm thinking, I'm either looking at things as they were or as they might be.

TIME   That's right, it is less real because it's either a memory in the past, or a fantasy in the future. So technically, because of that, neither one of me, the past or the future, really exists at all. Even the chronological sense you have of me is just a series of now.

ME   My mind is most of the time unfortunately either in the past or in the future. I see that most clearly when I am meditating, and it is very challenging, because the mind wants to go anywhere and everywhere apart from staying in the present. It's like I don't really want the present, the gift.

TIME   Very true, the present is a gift, but like you said, your mind is stopping you from having it.

ME   I believe the Indigenous people of Australia had no word for you.

TIME   That's right. What do you think that means?

ME   They must have been living in the present?

TIME   Maybe. Something you are struggling to do, and something that is causing you so much misery....Interesting eh?

55

TRANSFORMATION of SOCIETY

ME   Hello Transformation of Society, what do you look like?

TRANSFORMATION   I don't know yet because I haven't arrived!

ME   How can we create a new society, a beautiful society, a different society, a society that is peaceful, a society that is good for all, beneficial for all?

TRANSFORMATION   The thing is, for society to change, each one of you will have to change first, otherwise it will be the same old society but with different agendas. So the question needs to be, how do we ourselves need to change in order for society to be different? After all it's all of us that makes society isn't it? Ask yourself how transformation happens? Does it happen by dwelling on tomorrow? Does it happen by ruminating on yesterday? Does it happen by being present?

In the present moment when the bees are humming, the juice is flowing, the intenseness is lifting you out of the murk to send you soaring to the heavens. Is that when you receive the present, the present of transformation?

ME Of course that's it. I have noticed that you are experienced in moments of intense presence. The weird thing is that it doesn't seem to matter whether they are moments of extreme pain or moments of escalating ecstasy. When the focus is there you seem to arrive. It's like we somehow have to be lifted out of the ordinary to see a wider view, a bigger picture, sometimes a different picture altogether. So perhaps a better question would be, how do we get into the present moment?

TRANSFORMATION Ah ha, Good question. It's different for everyone. Life will show you the way if you allow it. The things that help are, taking responsibility, forgiveness, unconditional love, compassion, awareness, stillness, clarity of thought, discernment, willingness, meditation, good intentions, surrender, openness, passion, humility, the ability to see things as they really are, spending time in silence, and detachment from outcome.

ME I see. I was thinking we need a new vision for the future, an idea of how life 'should be', and then we could work towards it. I realise now that actually the important thing is the willingness to go on a journey, the journey into the present, into the intensity. To be able to sit in the intensity of silence, to savour it and to watch the changes is what we have to do.

TRANSFORMATION Yes. The experience is the key, thought is just a replay. You do not need to know in advance what is going to happen. Actually you cannot know in advance what is going to happen, you will know that when you get there, wherever and whenever that may be.

Right now you need an alert mind, a still mind, a focussed mind. An alert mind is silent, an alert mind is simply noticing and ready. The gift is always in the present, the truth is always in the present, love is always in the present.

ME And the gift is the truth and the truth is love. Love will show us the way.

TRANSFORMATION Yes, Love will be there for sure.

A FINAL NOTE

QUESTIONS AND THOUGHTS FOR THE AUSTRALIAN PEOPLE (AND ANYONE ELSE WHO IS INTERESTED) ABOUT OUR SITUATION IN AUSTRALIA

I keep hearing people talking on the media about reconciling our two cultures, The Indigenous People and The Non Indigenous People. How do we say sorry for what happened, and for it to mean something? How do we fix the situation of The Indigenous People? For it seems as though it is an unfixable situation. I have pondered much on this question, for I know life does not happen by accident, it happens *for* us, and not *to* us, and nothing is unfixable. Everything that happens is for us, is for our benefit. So with those thoughts in mind I have come to have more thoughts and ask more questions.

The Indigenous culture was a very aware way of life, connected to country, connected to nature. It nurtured its people, promoted wisdom, was sustainable for over 60,000 years, was happy, good for all, cost nothing, respected all beings and was in tune with everything around. It was a simple culture and yet profound. Going from accounts by some of the early settlers they were a happy, regal looking people who abided by the laws of the tribe and of the land. They walked the earth with sure-footed confidence, and had respect for all beings. There were many rites of passage members of the tribe went through as they grew up within the tribe. The men especially, went through massive amounts of physical pain and probably fear during some of their rites of passage and ceremonies, which would have afforded them great wisdom. I understand that facing fear and pain and going through them often results in more wisdom, more connection, more awareness and more empathy. And though they had lived this way for many thousands of years, everything was to change eventually, for that is one of the laws of the universe...... Change.

They were invaded. Their society was replaced only a comparatively short time later, by one that seems to be getting itself into quite a dysfunctional state. It is full of stress, has countless people with mental illness, has prisons full to overflowing and has lost to a large extent, its connection with nature. It is focussed on ownership of material possessions, has people who have nothing and others who own nearly everything. It has old people's homes filled with people who seem to have no knowledge of the art of dying and perhaps even living. All this together with the fact that most of the societies in this world, think it's perfectly excusable to go to war and try to wipe the other out.

However, it's not an accident their country was invaded, or is it? Do we attract what we need? If so, why did they attract so much ignorance, brutality and pain? For that matter why does anyone need pain and suffering? Does life happen by action/reaction? If we don't attract what we need, is life just one senseless experience? Had the wise ones of the tribes risen above their pain so much they didn't need to be here anymore? Did they know their time was up? Was it time for them to move beyond the physical world? Did they know they had to leave the others behind to go through whatever experiences they needed to have? Maybe they did for they were wise.

And what about the invaders, the ones who caused the pain? What drove them to do what they did? What fears did they carry within their hearts? What ignorance, greed and fear drove some of them to steal, decimate and try to destroy a people and their way of life? Were some of them compassionate? Were some of them brave? Did something go before to cause these tribal lands to be invaded? Was there a previous culture here, an ancient tribe who lived here a long long long time ago? Was Australia always an island or was it joined to another piece of land? How far back do you want to look? How big do you want the bigger picture to be?

We get so fixated on the small narrow part we can remember, or is recorded, and we forget it might have started way, way before. How many ancient cultures have inhabited this world? How many times do we have to come here to learn the lessons of forgiveness and unconditional love? Forgiveness of ourselves and of each other. There always has to be a bigger picture. What is yours?

ABOUT THE AUTHOR

Sally Patch was born in 1948 in England. She spent her childhood making and building things. After going to Guildford Art School in the late 60's to study photography she became a freelance photographer in London for seven years. Needing somewhere to live she bought a very dilapidated house and renovated it; building, that she had so loved in her childhood had reentered her life.

She had two sons, and in 1983 she decided to emigrate to Australia where she helped her brother in his business making unusual pottery. Eventually she started making her own sculptures and held sculpture classes in her home which she had built out of mud bricks.

In 1999 intense grief pushed her off her perch of comfort into an unexpected journey of self reflection and discovery. This led to a lot of volunteer work at places like Lifeline where the worked on the telephones, Paradise Kids where she became a buddy to children suffering from grief and loss, Hopewell Hospice, Headway, and eventually to the Vipassana Meditation Organisation.

This is her first book.

CONTACT ME AT

Website	www.sallypatch.com
Facebook	Conversations with Sally
Instagram	@conversationswithsally
Email	hello@sallypatch.com

FURTHER INFORMATION AT

Vipassana Meditation	www.dhamma.org
The Byron Katie Work	www.TheWork.com

FURTHER READING

'Loving What Is' by Byron Katie

ACKNOWLEDGEMENTS

I would like to give my heartfelt thanks to my two amazing editors Jillian Craig and Linda Munster for their ruthless honesty and enthusiastic support. Also Diana Razcek, Kate Patch, and Kat and Kurt Nischel for all their help and patience with my various IT struggles.